Praise fo
The Mystical Messiah

Alan Cohen has hit another home run! In this breakthrough
book, Alan gives us a new paradigm for our thinking as he
has dismantled old and limiting thought patterns about the
Bible. As a Fortune 500 executive, I know the importance of
applying metaphysical success principles to the marketplace.
Alan brings the teachings of Jesus into the understanding of
our everyday modern world. Through Alan's inspiration, Jesus
speaks directly to each of us personally, and to our spiritual
growth. An enormously insightful and introspective book.

—Dr. Richard Feller, MA, MBA, PhD,
author of *Fearless Wisdom*

This is a GREAT work!—much needed. Many of us feel
an intuitive connection to the master teacher Jesus, yet
find that the way many faith traditions articulate who
Jesus was, or what he taught creates a big disconnect in
our soul. In *The Mystical Messiah* Alan Cohen bridges
huge gaps and supports a greater connection to the man
Jesus and his teachings in a relevant and useful way. This
book and the wisdom within it, are a joy to behold!

—Dr. Michelle Medrano,
Lead Minister, Mile Hi Church

I love this book! It should be required reading for healers of all kinds. In my psychotherapy practice I see clients benefit immensely by applying holistic and spiritual truths to their lives. *The Mystical Messiah* demonstrates that Jesus was not only a spiritual master, but he illuminated deep psychological principles that change the lives of those who apply them. If you would like to get to the heart of your issues and profoundly heal them from the inside out, here you will find a treasure of tools that will accelerate your personal and spiritual growth in powerful and amazing ways.

—Day Singh, LCSW,
Psychotherapist and Holistic Life Coach

As a longtime student and teacher of *A Course in Miracles*, I know there is so much more to the teachings of Jesus than most people realize. I am thrilled that Alan Cohen has illuminated the metaphysical meaning behind Jesus's teachings. Like Alan, I see life as a series of parables that help us understand who we are, why we are here, and how to live. If you would like to understand your life from the highest perspective, this enlightening book will give you tremendous clarity and inspiration. *The Mystical Messiah* will find a welcome home on the bookshelves and in the hearts of everyone seeking miracles in their lives.

—David Hoffmeister,
author of *Awakening through A Course in Miracles*

Reading Alan Cohen's work is always a journey into profound wisdom, and *The Mystical Messiah* is no exception. Cohen's thoughtful look at Jesus and his teachings explores a deeper meaning of the Son of God, blending old stories with fresh understanding. This is a book to read again and again, as it guides us to live with greater Christ consciousness every day.

—Debra Landwehr Engle,
author of *The Only Little Prayer You Need*

As a trainer to self-employed professionals on taxes for over fifteen years and a practitioner of *A Course in Miracles*, I have experienced first-hand how overwhelmed many can feel about taxes. I am truly inspired by Alan Cohen's illumination of Jesus's advice on how to deal masterfully with taxes, exchanging the law of karma for the law of grace, and happily trading the disempowered feeling of "being taxed" for the peaceful, giving state of abundance. With quiet truth that rises far beyond worldly advice, Alan guides us to peace and prosperity in our finances and shows us how to fully integrate spirituality with our professional path. I could not recommend this book more highly.

—Maine Shafer,
Professional Tax and Business Advisor,
former Assistant Attorney General of New Mexico

As authors and relationship coaches, we read Alan Cohen's writings to each other first thing every morning as part of our daily spiritual practice. We find that this deepens our connection with each other. We love all of Alan's books, as they have a rare gift of reaching profoundly into our souls. In *The Mystical Messiah*, Alan introduces Jesus as a master guide to creating fulfilling human relationships. Alan skillfully and gently directs us to the very heart of what makes relationships work. Everyone who yearns to enjoy deeper connections with their loved ones will mine spiritual gold by reading this penetrating, transformational book.

—Dr. Anne Campbell, PhD (Neuroscience),
& John Campbell, MSc (Nautical Science)

Alan Cohen is a masterful author who teaches us that a shift in perception changes everything: Using metaphysical lenses to see Jesus as the great teacher he was and is; the True Light who enlightens us; the Spirit who makes all things new; the Giver of hope and Lover of all beings. This life-changing book will do what many of Alan's others book do so well—help readers move from fear to love.

—Peter Nieman, M.D.,
author of *Moving Forward* and marathon runner

In my role as editor of *Miracle Worker* magazine and
A Course in Miracles teacher for many years, I have found
The Mystical Messiah a truly inspiring book. It takes Jesus's
teachings to deeper levels. Anyone who wants to heal
their ego thoughts and awaken from the dream of fear,
separation, and death will find Jesus's spiritual principles given in this book invaluable. They have the power
to bring more love, peace, and happiness into your life,
and something you can share with all your relationships.
The Mystical Messiah is a transformational book that will
lead you out at the ego's prison and into the heaven within.

—Dan Strodl,
Editor, *Miracle Worker Magazine*

The experience of reading this book includes a simultaneous
and nurtured transformation. The timeless teachings of
Jesus Christ are so rich, one may accept such intellect and
awareness reserved solely for the son of God. Alan Cohen
articulates this is not true; all humans are perfectly designed
to "come forth!" and claim the promise of their unique talents.
The Mystical Messiah combines the author's mastery as a writer
and teacher so all healers, philosophers, and mystically-
inspired persons may be uplifted to the truth they seek.

—Debby Handrich,
Professor of Literature

ALSO BY ALAN COHEN

Are You as Happy as Your Dog?
A Course in Miracles Made Easy
Dare to Be Yourself
A Deep Breath of Life
A Daily Dose of Sanity
Don't Get Lucky, Get Smart
The Dragon Doesn't Live Here Anymore
Enough Already
Friends in High Places
The Grace Factor
Handle with Prayer
Happily Even After
Have You Hugged a Monster Today?
I Had It All the Time
How Good Can It Get?
Joy Is My Compass
Lifestyles of the Rich in Spirit
Linden's Last Life
Looking In for Number One
The Master Keys of Healing
My Father's Voice
The Peace That You Seek
Relax into Wealth
Rising in Love
Setting the Seen
Soul and Destiny
Spirit Means Business
The Tao Made Easy
Why Your Life Sucks and What You Can Do about It
Wisdom of the Heart

THE
MYSTICAL
MESSIAH

THE
MYSTICAL
MESSIAH

THE INNER MEANING
OF THE TEACHINGS OF JESUS

ALAN COHEN

ISBN: 978-0-910367-18-9
Ebook ISBN: 978-0-910367-37-0

Printed in the United States of America

To the mystical messiah,
who makes all things new

CONTENTS

INTRODUCTION

Jesus Christ has influenced the world more than any other person in human history. Though his feet trod the green hills of Galilee two millennia ago, to this day countless devotees recount his teachings, pray to him, heal by his power, emulate his life, build churches to his glory, sacrifice for him, and kill in his name. Others revile, deny, and mock him. If ever a man has rocked the world and redirected the course of life on Earth, it is the lone Nazarene.

Yet who among devotees and naysayers truly understands what this dynamic soul came to impart? Do preachers pierce to the heart of the truth he delivered, or is there a deeper meaning they overlook? Could there be more to the man and his message than we know?

We are most familiar with the religious Jesus, in whose name the sprawling faith of Christianity has been built. There is also the historical figure who learned carpentry from his father, disappeared for eighteen mysterious years, and then returned to preach to massive crowds until he was crucified. The political Jesus posed such a threat to the Hebrew leaders and Roman occupiers that they had to do away with him. The healer Jesus dispelled sickness, cast out devils, and raised the dead. The master psychologist Jesus explained why we suffer under the judgments we lay upon others. The liberator Jesus emphasized the spirit of the law over the letter of the law, and forgave offenders that others condemned. The punitive Jesus stormed the great temple and tore down the stalls of merchants—or was this the human Jesus, who lost his temper like the rest of us? The psychic Jesus identified John the Baptist as the prophet Elijah returned, and prophesied his own death and resurrection. Some researchers cite evidence of the yogi Jesus, who purportedly travelled to Egypt, India, and Tibet, where he studied in the esoteric mystery schools that prepared him for his momentous mission. More recently there is speculation about the family Jesus, who married Mary Magdalene, parented one or more children, and engendered a blood line that carries through to this day.

Yet amidst this dizzying array of roles there remains a little-understood Christ that could be the most important of all: the mystical messiah. Meet the visionary who imparted lofty truths so far beyond the comprehension of the simple people he addressed, that he had to cloak them in earthy parables they could grasp. This spiritual master shattered prevailing ideas of sin, declared ripe the harvest yet four months hence, and so compellingly denied death that deceased bodies rose and walked. He stripped the priests of hypocritical dogma and cryptically promised to rebuild the fallen temple in three days. Most important, he claimed his identity as a divine immortal being and called us to do the same. A bolder challenge was never posed.

A spiritual teacher asked a student, "Do you know the difference between you and Jesus Christ?" When the student sat silent, the teacher answered, "Jesus knows there is no difference." The mystical messiah came to level the playing field and meet us on common ground. Christ accomplished miracles because he understood the mechanics behind creation, and he rose beyond the illusions that keep humanity in bondage. He audaciously called himself the Son of God, and assured us that we are no less.

We are living in extraordinary times. The forces that drive humanity are intensified and accelerated. The darkness is darker, the light is lighter, and the contrast between the two grows sharper every day. While many people find comfort in traditional religion, others are reaching for more soul-satisfying truth. They are not content with a God who demands blood, incites war, and threatens infidels with eternal hell. Sincere seekers are striving to break free of guilt and acquaint themselves with a Higher Power that encourages joy rather than suffering. They yearn to find a foothold of safety amidst a world gone mad. We need to relate to a God who lifts, empowers, and heals us. The mystical messiah provided such a blueprint—but we must decode his brilliant metaphors to unveil it.

The book you are holding reveals the deeper meaning of the teachings of Jesus Christ, the grander truth he could not roll out because the people of his time were not ready to understand the spiritual subtleties his parables cloaked. The Nazarene planted seeds to sprout over the ages and bear fruit when the season became ripe. His teachings were time capsules, waiting for a more mature audience to unearth them. While a handful of visionaries in every generation have grasped the subtle meaning of Christ's teachings, there is now a groundswell of aspirants ready for esoteric discipleship. The sheer number of dedicated truth seekers is generating a tipping point of illumination. Not very long ago, people interested in metaphysics felt isolated, and had to carve their path behind closed doors. Now a legion of mighty companions walks by your side.

The path to liberation is not mysterious or reserved for a favored few. The ecstatic poet Rumi called enlightenment "the open secret." Truth stands before us like a gleaming jewel on a golden pedestal. Yet it seems elusive because we become immersed in trivial distractions. "Many are called but few are chosen" means that all receive the call, but few choose to hear it. If you are reading this book, you are ready to hear your calling. To some people, this book will remain invisible or unbelievable. To others, it will be a door to previously veiled dimensions that now reveal themselves in stunning splendor.

When we have exhausted all of our external journeys, the internal adventure will remain the only one that matters. A spherical Earth ensures that every circle you make around it will return you to the point of origin. Many people travel to Israel to follow in the footsteps of Jesus. Yet where his physical feet trod is not nearly as important as where his mind pointed. His kingdom, he affirmed, is not of this world. So why try to find him in a world he has outgrown? The mystical messiah beckons us to a far greater kingdom, constructed of empowered thoughts and a willing heart.

It is to this kingdom that this book is directed. Of the many Jesuses you know, one will take you all the way home. Let us now peel away the wrappings that enfold the master's teachings, and pierce to their core. We can shorten the time of wandering and suffering. Here you will find the formula that Jesus Christ used to achieve healing and miracles, that you may accomplish the same. Nothing would make Jesus Christ happier than for us to stand by his side knowing ourselves as the divine being he knew himself, and all of us, to be.

Let us begin.

MY COUSIN JESUS

After my first book, *The Dragon Doesn't Live Here Anymore*, was published, I was invited to deliver the keynote address at a national conference of Unity Church ministers in Missouri. As I stood at the podium about to begin my lecture, I remarked, "You might think it odd that a fellow named Cohen is giving a speech to a body of Christian ministers." I paused for effect, and then added, "But word has it that one of my relatives is very popular around here."

Likewise, you may wonder why that very fellow is writing a book about the inner teachings of Jesus Christ. "Are you a Jew?" you might ask. "A Christian? A Jew for Jesus? Or just mixed up?"

None of the above.

My relationship with Jesus is personal, not religious. I am not a member of the Christian religion, or any other. My church is the holy sanctuary of nature. I like Christian music that celebrates forgiveness and grace, but I turn it off when the singer extols the blood of the lamb. I understand Christ's teachings not through my intellect, but with my heart. He is my mentor, friend, and ultimate go-to when I have a question about what is real and how to live.

It wasn't always that way. I was born into a Jewish family that practiced the culture but not the religion. I slogged through bar mitzvah lessons and put up with distant relatives pinching my cheek at the reception. I swore I would never set foot in the temple again.

A year later, I received a postcard inviting me to a brunch for teenagers at my temple. I had absolutely no reason or desire to attend. Yet something inside me urged me to go. I now recognize that voice as the Holy Spirit guiding me to fulfill my destiny.

At the brunch I met a young rabbi, Stuie, the temple's youth director. He delivered an impassioned speech that moved me deeply. This man had a sincere, loving relationship with God. At the time, my family was living in a horrible inner-city neighborhood with many dark influences. I hung out in seedy environments with kids who were committing foul deeds and crimes. I was an awkward six feet tall at age thirteen, I wore glasses and braces, and I struggled with acne. Kids made fun of me, and my self-esteem was below zero. Rabbi Stuie was a ray of light in a horrid storm. He saw good in me and genuinely cared about me. In his presence I felt whole and valued. Stuie encouraged me to run for president of the youth group, and before long I was making speeches to the kids and adults, and leading prayers for the entire temple. His intervention in my life was an act of grace.

I became an orthodox Jew and observed all the very strict rules, prayed three times a day, and ate only kosher food—an intensive regime. Stuie helped me get a scholarship to a Jewish college where I studied the Bible in Hebrew and was not allowed to touch a woman. While my studies were initially inspiring, after seven years of practice, I began to feel suffocated and bored. The religion that once enhanced my life was now stifling it.

I took a bold step and left Judaism. I went into intense party mode and made up for all the fun I had missed as a religious teenager. I dated profusely, experimented with psychedelic drugs, sat at the feet of Hindu gurus, meditated with Zen monks, and went to every consciousness training I could find. What an exhilarating time of learning and growth!

During an intensive retreat at the Esalen Institute in Big Sur, California, I found a copy of the New Testament. As a Jew, this Bible had never come into my world. Jews did not talk about Jesus, so I had no relationship with him or his teachings. When I read the words of Christ printed in red, they leaped off the page into my soul. This man, whoever he was, uttered brilliant insights similar to the ones I had experienced under the influence of mind-expanding substances. The truth he spoke resonated within me at a cellular level.

Over the years my relationship with Jesus has deepened to the point that he has become my *sadguru*, the teacher of teachers who speaks most directly to my spirit, and whose guidance I most trust. I believe in him and his teachings more than the organization that has grown up around him. The Nazarene is my resource for spiritual guidance and comfort. Every day I thank God that Jesus came into my life and blesses me with his truth and grace.

One of the ways I connect with Jesus is that I see life through metaphors. Christ delivered his paramount lessons through parables, which I experience every day. Through *A Course in Miracles* and similar teachings, I see beyond the notions of sin, punishment, and damnation that oppress many people raised in traditional religions. In this book I intend to diffuse fear-based interpretations of Christ's message, and affirm the inherent beauty, worth, and innocence of us all. We might call this book a kind of "Jesus 2.0," a new iteration of a voice that echoes through the centuries for the upliftment of humanity.

Whether you are Christian, Jewish, any other religion, or no religion, Jesus speaks universal truth that can heal our lives. If you find value in Christianity, keep it as the wrapping for the wisdom he delivers. If religion bothers you, put it aside. If you have no relationship with Jesus, or judgments about him because you come from another religion, or you have had a bad experience in church, or you consider yourself an atheist, I would like to introduce you to the compelling voice I have come to know and love. Ultimately we must become less fascinated with Jesus the personality, and apply what he taught. The man was the messenger. The truth is the message.

Our journey has been long and at times hard and painful. Yet there is light at the end of the tunnel. A helping hand, by whatever name you know it, reaches from above to lift us. May we all receive the grace offered us, and shine as the lights of the world we were born to be.

A FEW NOTES
TO THE READER

The Words of Christ

In this book I quote many statements made by Jesus Christ as recorded in the New Testament. I have chosen not to include chapter and verse annotations for two reasons: First, many of his teachings are included in several different gospels, often with variations. There are also many different Bible translations. I prefer not to direct the reader to a particular chapter and verse, since there are numerous interpretations to choose from. Instead, I have sometimes synthesized several different gospels or translations to arrive at a statement that, in my opinion, offers the clearest description of Jesus's message.

My second reason for omitting annotations is that many readers have had negative experiences attending churches that constantly quoted chapter and verse, many of which underscore a punitive aspect of God. As a result, some people have developed an aversion to scripture. While all of the teachings in this book are based on scriptural accounts, I believe that the essence of a statement is more important than where it comes from, so I am presenting the statements to simply stand on their own merit.

With the Internet now at our disposal, a reader who wishes to find the source of a quote by Jesus can easily type it into a search engine and find many different references to it. I particularly like the website www.biblehub.com, which offers an exhaustive list of Bible translations and annotations, as well as many cross-references and interpretations.

A Course in Miracles

Here you will find many references to *A Course in Miracles*, a contemporary self-study program that opens the mind and heart to profound insights into spirituality, healing, relationships, forgiveness, and God. The Course was dictated by an inner voice that identified itself as that of Jesus Christ. In the Course, Jesus continues the teaching he initiated when he walked the Earth. He elaborates on the themes he set forth, and he clarifies messages that have become muddied or distorted through mistranslation or misinterpretation. Some people consider the Course a third testament and a correction for the mistaken notions that have grown up around Jesus and his message. To learn more about *A Course in Miracles*, visit the Foundation for Inner Peace, www.acim.org.

Contemporary Parables

Every chapter contains one or several anecdotes from my life or the lives of people I know, to support the theme of the chapter. As I recorded these stories, I realized that teaching parables are not exclusive to Jesus Christ. We all encounter and participate in parables each day, which yield us important spiritual lessons. The world "parable" comes from the Greek *parabola*, meaning, "side by side." A parable is a story with two meanings: an exoteric, or obvious meaning; and an esoteric, or more subtle meaning. When Jesus spoke of planting, reaping, baking, banquets, masters and servants, and wealthy business owners, he was delivering lofty spiritual truths in metaphors. We must unwrap the outer story to unpack the inner lesson. In that sense, all of life is a parable. It is my hope that the personal stories I share reveal their inner messages to you, and—even more important—you will build your own skill to more effectively interpret the parable that is your life.

THE BEGINNING
OF A MIRACLE

If you were a sixteen-year-old virgin girl and an angel came to you and told you that you were pregnant with the Son of God, how would you react? This was precisely the predicament in which young Mary found herself. This stunning announcement was further complicated by the fact that Mary was betrothed to Joseph, and to marry without virginity in those days was unthinkable—punishable even by death. The angel also informed Mary that her cousin Elizabeth, barren and beyond the age of motherhood, would also bear a child (who grew up to become John the Baptist).

There are two things you need to know about the Bible that will forever change the way you think about it. The first is that the events recounted in the Bible are more metaphorical than literal. The people and situations you read about represent ideas more than physical happenings. They are symbols of states of mind. To read the Bible as a material record only is to miss the core teaching it seeks to impart. The story is actually a progression of consciousness, dynamics unfolding in the minds and hearts of all people.

The second life-changing insight is that everyone in the Bible lives *within* you more than outside you. The Bible is not a story about things that happened to other people long ago. It is *your own story*, the momentous journey you are taking from fear to love, from alienation to connection, from brokenness to healing, from bondage to liberation, from death to life. You can read the gospels as your own personal journal.

All biblical stories teach us on three levels. The first and most obvious level is **interpersonal**, focusing on relationships *between* people, encounters that show us how to get along in the world and escape the hardships that burden humanity. In the famous parable, a man was beaten by thieves and left by the side of the road to die. Many people passed him without helping him. Finally, a Samaritan came along, took pity on the man, brought him to an inn, and told the innkeeper, "Take care of him until he recovers. I will pay his expenses." The story provides a dramatic teaching urging us to help each other in times of trouble.

Interpersonal Bible stories make good fodder for sermons and Sunday school lessons. You can't argue with "feed the hungry"; "let the one who is without sin cast the first stone"; and "forgive seventy times seven." Follow these rules, and the world will be a far more peaceful and harmonious place, closer to heaven than the hell it often is.

Yet there is more. The second level of teaching through story is **intrapersonal,** in which the characters and plot represent identities, traits, and beliefs that live within our own psyche. All biblical personages, including Moses, Pharaoh, Mother Mary, Jesus, the disciples, Mary Magdalene, Lazarus, Judas, and the rabbis and Romans who sent Jesus to the cross represent aspects of ourselves, acted out by *seemingly* external characters who express our own inner dynamics. Mary receiving the news that she was to bear the Christ child is really *you* recognizing your divine nature calling to be birthed into expression. *Your mind* is the womb in which God has planted the seed of divinity. Like Mary, you must decide if you are worthy to bear the Christ and if you will bring forth your inspired expression amidst critics and skeptics—who voice your own doubts and judgments. The arcs of biblical characters mirror your own evolution. Their biographies are your autobiography. While these characters appear to live in a distant time or book, they are not apart from you. They are disowned aspects of yourself, seeking integration and resolution.

Recognizing the Bible as a mirror allows us to reclaim the elements of ourselves that have been fragmented, and restore our wholeness. When you take your power back from the people and events to which you have ascribed unmerited authority, you attain the mastery you did not exercise when you believed the world was doing it to you or for you. You are doing it all to and for yourself.

In chapter 4, I will reveal the third and deepest level of Bible teaching. For now, these first two levels will give us plenty to absorb.

Angels Among Us

Just as Mary received the annunciation from an angel, angels also speak to us. They bring us guidance, healing, and hope. Some religionists tell us that miracles, angels, and divine intervention were reserved for days of yore, but have ceased in our time. *It is not so.* The Bible is not a milk carton with an expiration date. Truth is eternal, lest truth it would not be. Just as Mary, Jesus, his disciples, and the prophets were visited and guided by angels, so are you and I. If you are open to receive their aid, you will. If you do not believe in them, or you feel unworthy, or you busy yourself with distractions, you will not be aware of their presence and the gifts they offer. If there is any cut-off, it is not a date of biblical expiration. It is the way we cut ourselves off from the presence of love. Yet no matter how disconnected from the presence of love you have become, you can reclaim it, sometimes through miraculous events.

Recently divorced Ivy Olson had two small boys, no money, and a nearly empty refrigerator. Depressed and fearful, she had no idea how she was going to care for herself and her family during the holiday season. Then an older woman in her garden apartment complex invited Ivy and her sons for Thanksgiving dinner. The neighbor laid out a feast of Ivy's favorite foods, and demonstrated she knew things about Ivy that she could not have known. The woman sent Ivy home with leftovers that would feed her family for a week. The unconditional love this neighbor showed Ivy gave her faith that she and her boys were going to make it through this tough time.

The next morning, Ivy went to the woman's apartment to return some Tupperware containers. Ivy was shocked to find the apartment completely empty, without a stitch of furniture.

When Ivy went to the building manager to ask what had become of the woman, he told her that the apartment had been vacant for months. (YouTube: *Dinner with an Angel—It's a Miracle.*)

We, too, are being guided and sustained. Whether an angel whispers in your ear, or you have an uncanny intuition that proves itself, or the perfect person shows up at the right moment, you are being cared for by Grace. The same angelic source that spoke to Mary speaks to all of us and seeks to help us, if we are open to listen and receive.

Miracles in the Making

Mary represents the womb or space for the divine to enter the world. She is feminine, embodying the mystical, intuitive, invisible aspect of creation; she is young, innocent, and never touched by a man; and she is receptive. But the qualities of innocence, purity, youth, receptivity, and creativity are not restricted to young virgin women. Any person of any gender at any age or sexual experience can receive higher truth and generate visionary progeny that bless the world.

The angel of annunciation prophesied two seemingly impossible events: (1) a virgin would bear a child; and (2) a woman too old and barren to have a child would also give birth. This demonstrates that spiritual possibilities supersede the limitations to which the world subscribes. *A Course in Miracles* asks us to remember, "I am under no laws but God's." Ultimately nothing is impossible. I coach many women who are approaching age forty and fear that they are becoming too old to bear a child. Yet Hunza women in Asia are known to bear children into their mid-sixties. A recent news story introduced the world's oldest known father—an Indian man, age ninety-four. His wife and mother of the child is age fifty-three. When I took a trail ride in Hawaii, our guide showed us a private family cemetery containing the tomb of the patriarch who fathered a child when he was in his nineties. Age and its attributes are stories we make up. We are free at any moment to make up a new story.

We also hold untrue beliefs about disease. Every known disease has been healed in someone, and often many people. There is no such thing as an incurable disease. When we don't know what we can't do, we can override the limiting beliefs to which others subscribe. I know of a woman who wrote this note to her husband: "I never told you that the doctor called to report that you are infertile . . . Congratulations—it's a girl." When we hold firmly and faithfully to our vision, and do not allow ourselves to be stifled by false limits, we can transcend the *apparent* laws that govern people who are sick, poor, in pain, or apparently hopeless. Then we enjoy the benefits of the rock-solid universal laws that make us healthy, prosperous, and truly happy.

Really Immaculate

Physical virginity represents spiritual innocence. You are spiritually innocent regardless of your sexual activity or history. Your soul is pure no matter what you believe are your sins that would cause you to be punished or go to hell. In the mind of God, nothing you have done can cause you to become unworthy of love. Guilt and punishment are twisted stories that people make up. The word "gospel" comes from the Anglo-Saxon term "god-spell," meaning "good story." Stories of an angry, vengeful, punitive God who casts bad souls into hell for eternal damnation are not good stories. They are products of minds that have lost the awareness of their inherent innocence. When you remember your inviolate, untouchable, perfect purity, you reclaim your true nature.

One of my coaching clients told me that she suffers from "existential guilt," implying that guilt comes with existence. I had to laugh. There is no such thing as existential guilt. Guilt is the fabrication of a fearful mind, unnatural and alien to a divine being. God knows it not. Guilt is not an attribute of life; it is the opposite of life. I told my client, "Existence is innocent and so are you."

The word, "conception" means "idea." The deeper meaning of "immaculate conception" is "pure idea." The annunciation of the birth of Jesus represents the planting of a pure idea in your mind. Pure ideas are the ideas that God has about you and life, all of which are perfect. The immaculate conception is the vision of wholeness that God holds of all of us, and wishes for us to hold for ourselves. Forgiveness sees purity where fear laid condemnation. The real you has never been defiled, sexually or in any other way. Your true self remains fully intact as God created you. When you identify with innocence, you know yourself as God knows you.

Faith Justified

We can also learn from Mary's dilemma in telling Joseph that she was with child. What radical news to deliver to her betrothed! We are told that Joseph was initially upset, but eventually he came around to support Mary. We all face situations where we must tell people news about ourselves or our choices that may be surprising or hard for them to hear, and to which they may react with shock or resistance. But Mary had to do what she had to do. She trusted in the annunciation and she trusted in God. Her faith was justified when Jesus grew to become a world changer.

The seeds of higher vision that God plants in the womb of your mind will also turn out to be world changers. They may not transform masses of humanity, but they will transform your world. People stay in ruts not because they do not receive guidance, but because they do not act on the guidance they receive. In your quiet moments, God has spoken to your heart and given you messages that, when you put them into action, will uplift your life and the lives of those you touch.

If you do not believe you have received guidance, or you would like to receive more, simply sit quietly and ask to be shown what you are to do with your day and your life. It's hard to hear the voice of God when you are immersed in drama and distractions. But even a small effort to get still and listen will be rewarded. You may not hear a booming voice from heaven in that moment, but the planted seed will surely bear fruit.

When you act on authentic guidance, you do not need the agreement or support of other people. It's nice when that comes, but it is not required. Mary's faith did not depend on Joseph's response. You do what you have to do because you have to do it, and that is reason enough. No matter what you do, some people will agree and others will reject you. Even Jesus himself, the purest of souls with the noblest of intentions, found himself in a den of naysayers who felt threatened by him, and they reacted violently. But that did not stop Jesus from ful-filling his mission. He was perfectly authentic in his ministry, as you must be in yours. How you live is your ministry; you are always teaching by your example. Even if you never set foot in a church, you profoundly affect the world by your thoughts, words, and deeds. Never underestimate the value of your life. You are here for a high and holy purpose.

Call in Your Team

Because Mary is a part of you, you can call forth her innocence and faith to buoy you when you face a challenge. You can summon any biblical personage to edify any quality you wish to develop and manifest. You can activate the liberator Moses, the rock of faith Peter, or the innovator Abraham. Don't stop with Bible personalities. Invite to the party St. Michael, slayer of illusions, St. Francis, champion of the natural world, and Buddha, master of tranquility. You can also call upon the esteemed gurus and mentors that have touched you personally. All of these great souls are aspects of your own self. As you focus on their qualities of character, you make them real in your experience. You already *are* all that you see in them. It's time to take back the noble qualities we have projected onto apparently external personages, and claim the attributes of God as our own.

Mary had no idea where the angel's news would lead her. Neither do you and I recognize the doors that will open when we surrender to our inner calling. The annunciation is not a single event that happened to a chosen woman two thousand years ago. It is an ongoing communication between the source of love and all humanity. One moment of insight can change your entire life. Mary learning that she was to bear the Christ child was the beginning of an entirely new way of thinking that we can all step into. The blessed mother is not an icon to be venerated. She is an energy to be embodied. The biblical Mary said "yes" to her higher calling, and so will you. Love always finds a way.

THE STAR, THE SWORD, AND THE SAVIOR

When King Herod's astrologers informed him that a pow-erful Jewish leader was to be born under a new star in Judea, he ordered all male children under the age of two years to be killed. This is not the first time we have heard such a rash edict in biblical drama. In the Book of Exodus, when Pharaoh's advisors alerted him that a deliverer of the Hebrew people was imminent, he ordered all male babies to be slain. It was then that the mother of the infant Moses placed him in a reed basket and cast him onto the Nile to save his life. Later in Exodus, after God had exacted a series of plagues on Egypt, Moses threatened

Pharaoh that if he did not free the Hebrew slaves, the firstborn of Egypt would die, and they did.

If the Bible is a metaphor—as it is—and everything that happens in the Bible represents a dynamic within our own experience—as it does—what are we to learn from these savage acts?

The king and pharaoh in these stories represent the ego, the fear-based identity that rules our worldly experience. The ego, apparently sophisticated yet abysmally primitive, ostensibly powerful but frantically insecure, operates from one dictum: *maintain the status quo at all costs.* The way it is seems safe because it is known and controllable, even if the situation is horrid. So the ego defines all change as threatening, even if the change would liberate us. The ego, King Herod, and Pharaoh, rule *with* fear because they are ruled *by* fear. *Fortify the oppressed kingdom and get rid of anyone or anything that threatens it.*

The infants Moses and Jesus represent the advent of higher consciousness; the infusion of awakening into a world of massive dysfunction; rays of light in a dungeon of darkness. Both personages and the qualities they stand for deliver us from the tyranny of the limited known. In Exodus, Moses comes to liberate the Hebrew nation from centuries of slavery, representing long-entrenched habits of negative, self-defeating thinking. In the New Testament, Jesus comes to deliver the Jewish people from an overbearing religion and extricate humanity from the quicksand of guilt.

Pharaoh's and Herod's advisors represent the intellect, which interprets all incoming data in terms of whether it edifies or threatens the defended self. While the intellect can serve as a helpful guide when pointed toward noble purposes, when commandeered by fear it becomes a warmonger and resorts to primal defense and attack. Nothing frightens endarkened tyrants Pharaoh and Herod more than incoming light. So they take up their favored tool, the sword, and decree to obliterate any seed of change that might undermine their despotic rule.

In both cases, however, the protection of God and the tide of destiny are with Moses and Jesus. After Moses's mother casts him into the Nile, he is rescued by Pharaoh's daughter, who adopts him and raises him as her own son. So, in spite of Pharaoh's frantic efforts to rid his kingdom of insurrection, the crucial seed of change is planted in his own back yard. The wisdom of Spirit dispatches deliverance to the very heart of the site it most needs to transform.

In Jesus's drama, an angel guides Mary and Joseph to take the Christ child and flee to Egypt until King Herod dies. When the ego goes on a rampage, we must take refuge in an inner sanctuary until the insanity abates and it is once again safe to bring forth our spiritual nature.

The interpersonal dynamics of the Bible play themselves out as much today as they did when the story originally occurred. Political tyrants are threatened by voices of wisdom and freedom, so they banish, imprison, torture, or kill them. Hitler targeted the Jews. The horrid Laotian dictator Pol Pot, fearing educated citizens, ordered everyone who wore eyeglasses in that country to be killed. In America, people of color, minorities, and unfamiliar religions have been scapegoated. Abraham Lincoln, John and Robert Kennedy, and Martin Luther King, Jr. stood for social progress, which terrified old-guard people who had to do away with them. The non-violent Mahatma Gandhi was assassinated in India, as was Anwar Sadat in Egypt. While these dark acts were ostensibly political, their root cause is far simpler: fear is terrified by the light, and seeks to destroy it.

Dethroning the Inner Tyrant

Within your own life, whenever you step forward toward greater freedom or self-expression, a voice in your head seeks to thwart your forward movement. The inner Herod is threatened by you moving outside the circle of the known, and warns of horrible punishment if you defy your familiar pattern. When you seek to quit practicing your family's religion; marry someone of the wrong color, gender, age, or social status; take a job less prestigious than your ancestors; or start a risky business, the scaredy-cat part of your mind rears up like a lion and yells, "Don't you dare do this! Disaster is imminent!" But that voice is the liar. (Recommended: Zach Williams' song, "Fear is a Liar," available on YouTube) The lion king turns out to be the lyin' king.

There is also a Moses or Jesus within you that is destined to release you from bondage. It doesn't yell or scream like the tyrannical Pharaoh or paranoid Herod. It simply, quietly knows that you have a greater calling, and urges you to trust it. When you do, monumental transformation occurs.

A New Star in Your Sky

The new star in Pharaoh's and Herod's skies symbolizes the first glimmer of light, a harbinger of the healing coming to unshackle downtrodden humanity and liberate you from personal or group oppression. Darkness is not forever; there is always a turning point when the dawn reveals itself. Stars do not cause our experiences; they reflect inner dynamics. There is no authority in outer space; what we see at a distance but mirrors psychic configurations in inner space.

The three kings who saw the new star and followed it to Jesus's birthplace represent the wise elements of your intellect that recognize divinity. Smart leaders follow a higher star than politics, and so does the smart leader within you. Your greater self is more interested in uplifting humanity than achieving selfish ends. Worldly kings lay their gifts at the altar of a Higher King; then the ego, when tamed and trained, becomes a servant of the light.

Something inside you is always working its way toward the light. The three kings had to cross King Herod's borders to get to Bethlehem. Likewise, the Spirit within you must override the ego's boundaries to accomplish its mission. Ultimately the ego cannot stop the Spirit because the Spirit's power is real, and the ego's authority is fake.

All political borders are false and fabricated. If you look at the Earth from space, there are no lines printed on it that delineate one country from another. We make up stories of nationality, which all fall short of spirituality. There are no passports in heaven. When you are in, you are in, and no one needs to see a paper to verify that you belong in your right place.

The world has never dealt kindly with individuals who claim a divine identity. Fear rules humanity more than love. Yet, like tiny blades of grass grow to dislodge a huge block of a cement sidewalk, vision wields power that denial lacks. The rule of ego, like Herod, will ultimately fail. He was a crazy man who died. Christ is a sane spirit that lives. Let us not confuse the temporary with the eternal. One imprisons while the other liberates.

Narcissistic rulers come and go, but love endures forever. When illusions fall away, only truth remains. The star and the sword give way to the savior, the part of your mind that awakens you from dark dreams and remembers your mission to bring light to a world in deep need of healing.

3

THE QUIET CAVE

Joseph and Mary, nine months pregnant with Jesus, journeyed to Bethlehem for a census that required all Judean citizens to return to their hometown to be counted. This pilgrimage symbolizes that we must return to our Source to deliver the light within each of us. Our home is not a geographical location; we belong to a higher dimension. If you feel like you don't fit into the world, that's because you don't. No one really does. The world is more of a boarding school than a family residence. We have all fallen into the delusion that we are earthlings rather than angels. We are just visiting this planet.

There was a time when you were at peace with yourself and one with God. You existed without fear, pain, stain, or strain. Then the world encroached on you, and you forgot where you came from. The farther you drift from your Origin, the more you hunger to return. We are like the four-year-old boy who leaned into the crib where his infant brother lay, and begged him, "Please tell me about God. I'm starting to forget." We, too, retain the memory of our true home, and yearn to reclaim it.

Joseph and his family had to go home to be counted, and likewise you must find your way back to your original state. You have to be where you count. Identify with who God created you to be, not what the world has made of you. The Hebrew name "Bethlehem" means, "the house of bread," symbolizing the site of fundamental nourishment. The bread of physical life is grain. The bread of the soul is spirit.

No Room at the Inn

In crowded Bethlehem, Joseph and Mary could not find a hotel room. This symbolic predicament is just as real today as it was when Mary went into labor. The world does not have space for the Christ energy. Our days are jammed with substitutes for love and distractions from healing. Soul-depleting news, mindless busyness, and negative thought loops crowd inner quiet out of our experience. After years of social programming, the incessant noise in our head seems normal. So we accept it and we do not make space for peace. Meanwhile, a part of us knows that there has to be more to life than the one we've been living.

Filled hotel rooms represent chambers of your mind occupied by fear, guilt, obligation, stress, and unfulfilling goals. Think of your mind as a computer disk filled with data. We've all received a "disk full" message at one time or another. Then you have to erase old, irrelevant data to make space for new and more useful information. The world does not make space for peace. If you really want healing, you will have to find it in a place other than where the masses occupy.

A Way in a Manger

After Joseph and Mary failed to find a room in crowded Bethlehem, a kind woman guided them to a cave just outside the city. We are told that the place was a manger, softened by straw, surrounded by friendly animals. You are familiar with the scene.

The Son of God was born not amid pomp and glitter, but simplicity and humility. The Christ within us does not seek or care for the fanfare of the world; quality of life is more important than social climbing. Ultimately the ego must relinquish its demands and let nobler values guide. Do you really have to fight for what you think you need? Or can you quietly trust that your good will show up in the perfect way and timing as you relax and turn your welfare over to the Higher Power that loves and cares for you?

It's hard to retain inner peace when we get caught up in worldly power games. This is why so many celebrities sadly die at a young age of various addictions, murder, or suicide. They stepped into vast money, fame, doting groupies, sexual opportunities, and people who see them only for what they can get from them. Very few people have the strength of character to handle such avalanches of attention and influence. Just a handful of people in Hollywood or politics are mature enough to keep their head above such turbulent waters. Abraham Lincoln said, "Nearly all men can stand adversity, but if you want to test a man's character, give him power."

When Jesus Christ reached adulthood, he retained the humility that characterized his birth. He remembered, "It is not I, but the Father within me who does the work." Jesus was clear that he was a vessel through which the Source poured blessings to the world. This is the ego emptiness we must embrace if we are to be effective teachers, leaders, or healers, and avoid the traps into which so many fall.

The Birth of a New Consciousness

The birth of Christ is an event of awareness more than a physical occurrence. Christ was not absent and then became present. Christ is always here. The body comes and goes, but Spirit is eternal. Jesus's physical birth represents our acceptance of the presence of love, the initial recognition of God as our true Self.

The small mind, which thrives in the illusion of time and reinforces it, tricks us into believing that the birth of Christ happened at a specific moment along a lengthy timeline from which we are separated by two millennia. That is true only at the shallowest level of biblical teaching. Christmas is an ongoing event that shines far beyond the holiday or even Christianity. All religions celebrate light as a symbol of the presence of God in the world. Hannukah is the flame that burns within you far beyond the limits that time would lay over it. Diwali, celebrated by Hindus, Jains, and Sikhs, represents the victory of light over darkness. Buddhists honor the birth of Buddha, whose name means "the enlightened one." Ultimately all spiritual paths lead us from night to day, from illusion to truth, from dreaming to waking. Jesus and other spiritual masters are not out there somewhere. They are in here, everywhere.

Coming Home to Wholeness

God did not come into the world once as a baby. God comes to the world through every baby. If you can see Christ in the eyes of your child—or any child of God—you reenact the nativity. If you can see Christ in your own eyes, you reenact the resurrection.

If you recognize Jesus as God walking the earth as a man, you are accepting that God also walks the earth through you. Christ pleads with you not to separate yourself from him or see his story as distinct from yours. They are one and the same. Jesus calls not for devotees, but for equals. If you see God in Jesus but not yourself, you have missed the essence of his teaching. We enter heaven arm in arm or not at all.

When you regard the Bible less as a history and more of a personal journal, the people in the Bible cease to be characters, and they become *characteristics* of yourself. So it is with all stories you look upon that seem to be outside you, but are really reflections of your psychic undercurrents. You are not in the world. The world is in you. The star, the sword, and the savior are aspects of your own psyche. Every event in the Bible, in your dreams, and in your life is an invitation to reclaim your wholeness. The Bible a looking glass. When we can look in the mirror and see God, we have attained the vision the Bible was given for us to attain.

IN MY FATHER'S HOUSE

When Jesus was twelve years old, his parents took him to Jerusalem, where he wandered off and they lost track of him. Joseph and Mary anxiously searched for their child for three days, to no avail. Finally they found him in the great temple, teaching a group of learned men. He was lecturing with such authority that the scholars were amazed.

The couple approached Jesus and asked him, "Why did you treat us this way?" He answered, "Did you not know that I had to be in my Father's house?"

This incisive question brings us to the third level of Bible understanding: the *transpersonal*—the spiritual dimension that goes beyond the physical and psychological planes. Jesus was bold enough to tell his earthly parents that his real Father was God. Likewise, your physical parents are not your original parents, nor are your children your own. Worldly parents represent the role of God, but our true Source soars far beyond genetics. Our divine identity surpasses body, personality, and cultural conditioning. Our real attributes are those of Spirit.

There is so much more to us than the world recognizes! *Star Wars'* Yoda wisely stated that we are luminous beings, not crude matter. We are created in the image and likeness of an all-powerful, infinitely loving, perfect God. Any lesser identity does not befit us.

Many Christians believe that Jesus Christ was the only son of God, and the rest of us are miserable sinners cast out of the kingdom Christ proclaimed. Nothing could be further from the truth. Jesus was not an exception to the destiny of humanity; he was the *fulfillment* of it. He is not our superior to be idolized, but a role model of the potential of which we are all capable. Jesus is our elder brother who has trod the path to liberation we all walk, and mapped the way for us to join him. Now he lingers a while to show us the way out of the hellish world we have manufactured. He extends his hand to lift us to our rightful place beside him. Christ foretold, "Even greater things than I, shall you do." If we are less than Christ, how could we achieve greater feats than him?

Who is Really Crazy?

The very statement that yields humanity entrée to the kingdom of heaven is the one that got Jesus crucified. The Hebrew elders felt severely threatened by his claim to be the son of God, just as many are frightened today if someone makes a similar assertion. If you stepped up to a pulpit of a church or synagogue, wore a name tag at a business meeting, or went to a family dinner and proclaimed, "I am the holy son (or daughter) of God," you might be mocked, shunned, or put away. Claiming to be one with God is the ultimate blasphemy in the kingdom of fear. People committed to misery are threatened by love. But misery has enough company. Love needs more.

If you believe you are the *only* son of God, you are also deceived. We are all equally God, no one the embodiment of superior holiness. In 1959, a mental institution in Ypsilanti, Michigan housed three patients who each claimed to be Jesus Christ. In a clever experiment, social psychologist Dr. Milton Rokeach brought the three men together to find out what would happen when they encountered each other. In his book *Three Christs of Ypsilanti,* Rokeach commented that the patients were "confronted with the ultimate contradiction conceivable for human beings: more than one person claiming the same identity." The result? Each of the Christs thought he was the only savior, and argued with the other two.

Yet the psychologist's comment is as revealing as the experiment itself. He believed that only one person could be the Christ, which makes him as deluded as the patients. Actually, *more so.* At least the three patients had some sense that they could be the Christ. Rokeach believed that he could not. People who claim to be God are generally assumed to be crazy. Yet people who claim not to be God are crazier. The body, personality, or ego is not God. The Spirit that shines through us is.

The World's Greatest Lover

In the brilliant film *Don Juan de Marco,* a near-suicidal young man claims to be Don Juan, the world's greatest lover. He is apprehended, institutionalized, and assigned to a psychiatrist whose life has become devoid of passion. As the psychiatrist attempts to rid the patient of his fantasy identity, he realizes that Don Juan is living a far richer life than his own. Over time, the patient's vitality seeps into the psychiatrist's psyche, the elder is restored to joy, and his long unfulfilling marriage is resurrected. Eventually the psychiatrist playfully becomes a disciple of Don Juan, and joins him as one of the world's greatest lovers.

We might say that, spiritually speaking, Jesus was the world's greatest lover in that he brought a love to the world that far transcends what most people call love. He told us, "I have loved you with an everlasting love." Most "love" is not everlasting. It is conditional. "If you build your world around me, I will love you." "If you agree with me about how to raise our kids, I will love you." "If you join my religion, I will love you." Then, the moment the other person fails to meet our expectation, the "love" is out the window. What appeared to be love was a fictitious need based on the erroneous idea that we are empty and lacking.

When we love as Jesus did, we join him as the world's greatest lover. Christ does not seek disciples. He seeks peers. The mystical messiah's goal was not to glorify himself. It was to elevate his audience so we share the higher ground upon which he walked.

I enjoy watching videos of Bob Ross, the gentle artist who for many years taught a wildly popular painting class on public television. I am amazed at the stunning landscapes Bob created during a twenty-six-minute show. If ever there was an example of Spirit breathing greatness into the world through an open, kind-hearted soul, it is Bob Ross.

I was touched by a comment about Bob posted by a YouTube viewer: "He didn't paint to show how good of a painter he was. He painted to show how good of a painter you can become."

Jesus Christ didn't walk the Earth to demonstrate how special he is and how sorrowful we are. His mission was not to make himself the star of the movie. His mission was to turn a horror movie into the greatest love story ever told, and cast us all in leading roles.

Your True Family of Origin

Jesus's claim of God's fatherhood overturns the meaning of "family of origin," which usually refers to the biological family into which you were born. Our true origin goes back much farther than the birth of the body. The beginning of your body was not your beginning, and the end of your body is not your end. Your spiritual nature extends far beyond these arbitrary bookends. The real you was never born and will never die. Your true self is eternal. "What is born of flesh is flesh. What is born of spirit is spirit." Your body was born of flesh. Your soul has a far vaster source and destiny.

A student who had been abused as a child and felt stuck in that pattern told the spiritual teacher Abraham, "You can't teach an old dog new tricks." Abraham replied, "You have no idea what an old dog you are." Your true self runs far deeper and stronger than any programming you picked up as a child. Your spiritual nature can overcome any human experience. Psychology operates at the level of personality; Spirit penetrates to the soul. When we recognize and claim our divine identity, we gain the leverage to heal any adverse psychological or physical condition.

Mind Your Business

In some biblical translations, Jesus told his forlorn parents when they found him in the temple, "I had to be about my Father's business." This sheds an entirely different light on what we call "business." Many of us feel pressured or overwhelmed by our job, even addicted to it. We huff and puff on a hamster wheel, repeating a stifling daily grind and making little or no progress. As a result, we become stressed, depressed, or sick. That's because what we call "business" is not our real business. Our true vocation is to live from our spirit. Any activity that magnifies our joy is in harmony with our destiny. Any activity that squashes joy runs contrary to our purpose. Your mission in life is not a material achievement; your mission is a state of mind.

Engaging in worldly business does not preclude being about your Father's business. Your day job can serve as a venue to bless and heal. A café near my house offers free breakfast to homeless people every morning. In St. Louis, a policeman was called to a Walmart store to arrest a woman who had been caught shoplifting. When he learned that the woman was living homeless in her car with her four children, he went into the store and purchased food for her family. Many schoolteachers, strapped by low school system budgets, buy supplies for their students out of their own pockets. When a clerk at the drive-thru window of a fast-food restaurant saw one of his customers in tears, she explained that her husband had died the previous night. The clerk called the kitchen staff to the window, and they shared a moment of prayer for this woman. Our day job is not an exception to Jesus's teaching to remember God; it is the fulfillment of it.

The Secret Location of the Great Temple

When Jesus asked Joseph and Mary, "Did you not know that I had to be in my Father's house?" was he implying that the great temple of Jerusalem is the home of God? Or is the real home of God the Vatican, Mecca, the Bodhi Tree, the Great Pyramid of Giza, Machu Picchu's Temple of the Sun, Ayer's Rock, or the Sedona vortexes? It is all of these, and none. The great temple dwells *within* us. You take the temple with you wherever you go. God's church is not confined to a city, building, or mound. It is a state of consciousness you enter through the door of a pure heart. The mystic Persian poet Kabir said, "Wherever you are is the entry point."

Jesus's first teaching was his ultimate teaching. We must find our way to the inner temple and be about the business that brings us true reward. The world will chide us when we do not bow to its demands, but we cannot afford to linger where we don't belong. Joseph and Mary considered Jesus lost when he departed from his worldly family's activities, but he was really found. Likewise, your family or friends may consider you lost when you are no longer interested in the goals and activities they hold dear. At some point the trinkets of the world lose their glitter. You value living true to your guidance more than justifying your existence to insecure people. Your family may try to influence you to get a secure job, buy that expensive house in a posh neighborhood, or give up your silly woo-woo practices. Yet once you have tasted a grander reality, Smallville loses its appeal. The genie is out of the bottle, and you can't squeeze him back in. The world is not your business. Heaven is.

THE LOST YEARS

The New Testament accounts for the life of Christ until he was twelve years old, and then lapses until Jesus began his ministry at age thirty. What was Jesus doing during those crucial eighteen years? Was he working as a carpenter? Practicing the Jewish religion? Or was he, as some claim, immersed in intensive esoteric training to prepare him for the staggering role he was to assume?

There is a great deal of speculation, supported by a certain amount of evidence, that Jesus journeyed beyond the land of Judea to study with metaphysical masters associated with ancient mystery schools. Some historians say that he traveled to Egypt, others cite sojourns in India and Tibet, and others suggest that he was holed up with the Essenes, a reclusive sect that sought to live the spirit of the law rather than labor under its letter.

If the life of Christ symbolizes our own journey—as it does—to understand his "lost" years, we must consider a phase of life when we, too, disappear from the world we have known, and establish a new life at a higher frequency. The path the world prescribes for you is not your ultimate destiny. There is a loftier dimension that will bring you richer reward. While it is possible to merge a physical and a spiritual life, at the outset of soul exploration we must step back from worldly pursuits and dive deep within.

This crucial course correction often takes the form of a lifestyle change. You might quit your job, leave your relationship, forge distance from dysfunctional relatives, or move to another city. You might purify your diet, take up yoga, or develop your healing skills. You may study with a spiritual master, join a community, or retreat to an ashram or nature sanctuary. While some people call such a purposeful step "dropping out," you are really dropping *in*. You are mobilizing physical changes in the service of spiritual advancement.

Horizontal change moves you from one job you don't like to another job you don't like, or from one painful relationship to another, or from one unsatisfactory living situation to another. But geographical movement does not ensure spiritual advancement. Ernest Hemingway said, "Never mistake motion for action." Just because you are doing something doesn't mean you are getting somewhere; much of worldly activity is just spinning our wheels.

Vertical change ascends to a new state of mind. The real journey is one of consciousness. The worldly plot is the *story line*. The spiritual plot is the *glory line*. We engage in both plots simultaneously. In the end, worldly activities return to dust. Yet the lessons we learn along the way stay with us forever.

Retreat time is one of the most direct ways to align with your spirit. To master the world, you have to disappear from the world. You are not disappearing into oblivion, but rather stepping into a more substantial realm invisible to the world. You are not losing your life, but gaining greater life. Jesus said, "Whoever wants to save his life will lose it, but whoever loses his life for my sake will find it." Here is a perfect example of how a strictly literal interpretation of Jesus's teaching falls short of the deeper meaning he intended to convey. He was not requiring the physical death of his followers, but rather letting go of an old way of living to make way for a new and better one. The more you cling to a life you have outgrown, the more your energy will dissipate. When, instead, you walk your authentic spiritual walk as Jesus walked his, the more your energy will increase. You are giving up nothing to gain everything.

All great spiritual masters retreated so they could connect with higher guidance. Jesus went into the desert for forty days. When Moses was banished from Egypt, he wandered in the wilderness for many years before he found God on Mount Sinai. Mohammed withdrew to a mountain cave, where he received the Quran. Like these spiritual giants, you will not find God amidst the busyness and distractions of the world. A quieter place reveals the gateway to heaven.

The Gifted Return

Mythologist Joseph Campbell mapped "the hero's journey" we all take. A striking insight or unexpected event dislodges you from your known life, and you set out on the quest to overcome your challenge or gain enlightenment. You gather allies, encounter foes, and undergo tests and trials. Eventually you conquer your fears and you claim the pearl of great price—a higher state of consciousness.

But the journey does not end there. Once you have attained greater learning, you must come back to share your insights with others who stand at an earlier stage of the path you have tread. The Holy Grail is not a physical chalice. It is the wisdom you gain through overcoming adversity or receiving a stunning awakening. This is your gift and legacy to the community. Real teachers don't acquire wisdom and then disappear. They return to help others.

Jesus had to come back from his eighteen retreat years because he had a mission to fulfill. His disappearance would have been meaningless without a reappearance. So it is with your journey. You must extend to others what you have gained. We never learn just for ourselves. *A Course in Miracles* reminds us, "When I am healed I am not healed alone." Your awakening is not just for yourself; it is for many.

If you have gone through a health challenge, relationship breakup, abusive situation, or financial crisis, the ordeal may knock you out of circulation for a while. You must go into a cocoon to regroup and heal. Yet the entire experience leads to the greater service you will ultimately provide. Your absence from the world leads you to greater presence in the world.

If you wish to develop your Christ-like qualities, use your down time to energize your up time. Step away so you can step up. No one knows exactly what Jesus was doing during those eighteen "lost" years, but one thing is for sure: he was using them to become found. None of your time is lost. Every moment is leading to something better. When we are in the trenches, it's hard to see how difficult experiences fit into the greater picture. But they do. Like Jesus and other spiritual heroes, you, too, will return with a gift for a waiting world.

A VOICE IN THE WILDERNESS

The first we hear of Jesus after his mysterious hiatus is his meeting with John the Baptist, an impassioned prophet who cleansed masses of penitent Judeans with water. At the destined moment, Jesus approached John, fell to his knees in the shallows of the Jordan River, and asked to be baptized. John recognized Jesus as the messiah and told him, "It is I who should come to you to be baptized." Jesus replied, "Let it be so now, for we must do all that God requires."

John's reticence to baptize Jesus symbolizes the part of your mind that hesitates to play your key role in ushering Christ into the world. Jesus' response reminds you that you have a divine destiny as a venue for God to be present with us.

Baptism is far more than a physical act. We must wash away old, limiting, encrusted beliefs before we can step into a more expanded world. Jesus later said, "You must be born again before you can see the kingdom of God." Such rebirth is the result of a shift in perception. Visionary poet William Blake said, "If the doors of perception were cleansed every thing would appear to man as it is, infinite." Being born again means to become a new person because we are choosing new thoughts. Real baptism is a transpersonal experience in which erroneous beliefs and experiences are rinsed, leaving us with clear recognition of our original innocence.

The Power of One

John the Baptist lived sequestered in the desert, surviving on locusts and wild honey. He was the original dropout. When perplexed Judeans asked John who he was, he answered, "I am a voice crying out in the wilderness." John represents the portion of humanity that has awakened and calls their slumbering brethren to stir. While all people embody the divine, only a portion of humanity realizes it. Most minds are consumed with fear, mayhem, disaster, doom, and death. The world is a wilderness of the weird, with but a few voices heralding a lusher, greener reality.

Intrapersonally, John signifies the voice within you crying out for truth amidst the sprawling desert of illusions. While all kinds of voices speak in your head, many of them negative, there is one within the racket that stands for sanity. The goal of your spiritual path—and your entire life—is to remember your spiritual identity and live your divine purpose. But first you must bypass the temptation to believe you are lacking, unworthy, or doomed to failure. When you hear and follow the inner teacher, you find solace that nothing in the world can offer.

A Course in Miracles promises,

> Each hour that you take your rest today, a tired mind is
> suddenly made glad, a bird with broken wings begins to sing,
> a stream long dry begins to flow again. The world is born
> again each time you rest, and hourly remember that you
> came to bring the peace of God into the world, that it might
> take its rest along with you.

John the Baptist is not a remote biblical personage. His
essence lives within you, exhorting you to claim your divine
destiny. John's famous exhortation is "repent." Since many of
us have been browbeaten by bible-thumping preachers and
annoying proselytizers, we may be prone to turn off when we
hear that word. But if you know the origin of the word, it makes
sense and becomes attractive. The word derives from the Greek
metanoia, which means "a change of mind." To repent is to turn
away from the belief that you are a guilty sinner, and remember that you are inherently pure and absolutely beloved of your
Creator. Your inner healer reveals the spiritual gold within you.
You are not here to change the world. You are here to change
your mind about the world. A vision upgrade will achieve what
anxious effort cannot.

The Light within the Darkness

When John recognized Jesus amidst the crowd of normal
people, he represents the part of you that is aware of your true
self, and that of others, standing out amidst a crowd of lack-
luster extras. The imposters are the false identities we have

accepted—our sense of smallness, limitation, vulnerability, and guilt. Even while those imposters clamor for our attention and demand that we heed their reality, our innate perfection shines.

When you accept your wholeness, you recognize the wholeness within everyone. Enlightenment is a package deal. Everyone is included, no one left out. The vision that John the Baptist used to recognize Jesus is the same vision that enables us to recognize the Christ within ourselves and others. Real seeing comes when we use Spirit's eyes. All of our experience in life depends on the vision we use.

Another Voice in the Wilderness

Before Jesus began his ministry, he retreated to the desert, where he fasted and prayed for many days. During that time, we are told, the devil hurled three temptations at him. The devil is not a little red half-man, half-animal with a goatee, horns, pointy tail, and trident. What people call "the devil" is more like the Buddhist idea of *Maya*—illusion. There are not two powers in the universe. There is one power—God. Yet we can take the power that God has given us to create with our mind, then think erroneous thoughts, and manufacture experiences that cause us to suffer. The devil is nothing more than wrong thinking. We defeat the devil by replacing erroneous thoughts with higher truth.

When Jesus grew hungry, the tempter told him, "If you are the son of God, turn these stones into bread." Jesus replied, "Man does not live by bread alone, but by every word that proceeds from the mouth of God." He was affirming that we are spiritual beings more than material beings. Food alone will not sustain us. Our true nourishment is our spiritual connection.

The voice of illusion then challenged Jesus to throw himself off the highest point in the temple, and order angels to catch him. Jesus answered, "It is written, 'Do not put the Lord your God to the test.'" Jesus was facing the original daredevil. The lesson is simple: Don't do stupid things to prove you are spiritual. Be smart. Real spirituality is as practical as it is visionary.

Finally, the sneaky one took Jesus in a vision to a high mountain and showed him all the kingdoms of the world in their glory. "This can all be yours if you worship me," he promised. This is perhaps the most relatable of the temptations, akin to Darth Vader trying to coerce Luke Skywalker to join the dark side of the Force. Seeking worldly glory is a form of worshipping the devil. When you give your power to amassing stuff, social recognition, power, and fame, you are in for a very rough ride. The glitter of the world soon fades, and it is reforged into the bars of a golden cage. Jesus answered, "Worship God and serve Him only." You can't simultaneously have faith in Spirit and in stuff. You can have stuff and enjoy it, but you can't afford to let it run your life. Only the Source of all blessings is worthy of our reverence.

This scenario is another perfect demonstration of the intrapersonal nature of the Bible. All of these temptations occurred *within* Jesus's mind. He was not wrestling with an external person or force. He was grappling with beliefs in his own psyche. And so it is for all of us. While we seem to be battling external entities, we are really dealing with internal dynamics. The entire spiritual journey occurs within.

When Rebels Become Heroes

Voices in the wilderness like John the Baptist and Jesus overcoming *Maya* are usually mocked, shunned, and crucified. Yet after the masses are done laughing, rejecting, and destroying them, their ideas catch on and they are glorified. The outcasts of one generation become the heroes of the next. The Catholic Church sentenced Galileo to lifetime house arrest for his heretical assertion that the Earth revolves around the sun. President Theodore Roosevelt refused to electrify the White House because he worried that it would cause a fire. The father of Orville and Wilbur Wright was a preacher who declared that their experiments with air flight were the work of the devil. The ego fears any diversion from the familiar, even if the change could bring a vast improvement. In spite of initial fear-based resistance, astronomy, electricity, and air travel have become boons to humanity. What starts out as a voice in the wilderness grows into a garden of blessing.

The world is a maze of false ideas, cleverly laid one upon another to make them appear solid, integrated, and impenetrable. Yet there always comes along an innocent child who shouts to the crowd, "Look, the Emperor is not wearing any clothes!" Voices in the wilderness poke holes in the deceptions of the world, just as a voice in your head leads you to dismantle the illusions that have distracted you from love. When we allow the cleansing water of truth to wash away the scales that have covered our eyes, we see clearly, and the world is born anew.

IN THIS DAY

Soon after Jesus was baptized, he showed up at the temple in Nazareth, the town where he grew up. He is now a vibrant man thirty years of age, slim yet strong, his eyes shining and his demeanor compelling. He volunteers to read from the Torah, citing a prophecy of Isaiah: "The Spirit of God is on me . . . to proclaim freedom for the prisoners and recovery of sight for the blind, to set the captives free." Jesus completes the reading, sets the scroll down, scans the congregation, and proclaims, "In this day the scriptures are fulfilled."

A gasp rises from the crowd, ricocheting through the old synagogue like a small earthquake. "Blasphemy!" an elder cries out. "How dare you utter such a profanity!" shouts another. "The scripture will be fulfilled only when the messiah comes!" Amidst a tempest of indignation, the son of Joseph the carpenter, no longer welcome in the orthodox assembly, is ejected from the temple onto the street. This incident signifies the beginning of Christ's rejection by critics.

Jesus's statement is radical because we have been taught that the kingdom of heaven is just around the next bend or on the other side of the grave. Happiness will come one day, but surely not today. You will become enough when you find your soulmate, have a baby, receive a promotion, get your book published, win the lottery, or accomplish another just-beyond-reach event. When we finally achieve the goal, we feel a momentary rush of happiness. But soon emptiness again creeps into our gut, promising that the next goal will *really* fulfill us. And so we go on, chasing a carrot dangling on a stick just outside our grasp.

Jesus's heretical proclamation represents the part of your mind that recognizes that the good you seek is available now. Somewhere deep inside, you understand that there is nothing you need to do first to become worthy of the kingdom of heaven. The deservingness you have struggled to earn is already hard-wired into your soul. If you have a hard time accepting the purity of your soul, it's because your self-doubts—represented by the scoffing members of the synagogue—have been shouting so loudly that your inner messiah has been drowned out. Your self-judgments have gruffly tossed you out of your internal temple of peace, onto the street of adverse public opinion, to wander and wonder why you can't seem to get it right.

But the Christ in you, your illuminated self, is not daunted. It knows the truth of your divine nature. Even though that radiant presence is rejected by small-minded people and elements of your own mind, your inner messiah is established in perfect enoughness. The light that you are does not require approval by the world. Its nature is simply to shine.

While humanity seeks, Christ finds. To accept Christ's message of uncompromised sufficiency is the pivotal moment in a soul's evolution, the turning of the corner onto the path that leads us home. When Jesus declared, "In this day the scriptures are fulfilled," he did not mean only the day on which he spoke those words. Today is that glorious day if you are willing to let it be.

Hometown Disadvantage

In sports, the home team has an advantage over the visiting team. On the spiritual path, the opposite is true. People who knew you as a child are less likely to accept your spiritual gifts than those who met you as an adult. Even people who knew you as a younger adult may be unwilling to recognize that you have changed and grown. As Jesus departed from the synagogue after being spurned, he noted, "A prophet is never honored in his home town."

Of course not. Your mother changed your diapers. Your father told you to stand up straighter. Your music teacher put up with you hitting clunkers on the piano. Your orthodontist straightened your crooked teeth. Your priest heard your confessions. Your family, old friends, teachers, doctor, and clergy still think you are twelve years old—and they probably always will. Very few messiahs escape judgment by those who remain chained to their own daunting past. Smart saviors don't bang on their schoolmates' doors for approval.

But you are not the same person you were when you were pudgy and pimpled. You would not repeat what you did before you knew better. Your values have changed and you have grown, transformed, and in many ways healed. You have developed new skills and gifts you deliver to the world. How sad if you denied your passion, talent, and vision because people who once knew you don't acknowledge you now. Jesus was not put off by the temple congregants' rejection. He understood that their criticism was not due to his inferiority, but their poor self-images projected onto him. They could have allowed him into their hearts, accepted his magnitude, and been blessed by the presence of God as he lived, breathed, and walked among them. But they were not ready.

Some people in your life recognize your extraordinary gifts, and others do not. Don't let those who misunderstand you stop you from delivering your talents. When Jesus later sent his disciples out to teach and heal, he advised them, "When anyone does not welcome you, shake the dust off your feet and move on."

Healing the Inner Critic

It's one thing to leave behind people who judge you. The deeper work is to leave behind the inner critic. If a criticism by another person bothers you, a part of you must agree with it. Your parents or other significant influencers may live in a different city or have passed on; yet you have absorbed their negative voices as if they are your own. Healing those discouraging disapprovals is an inside job. It is not other people's approval you need to gain. It is your own.

Facing and overcoming painful criticism is a golden opportunity to free yourself from the lies that have shackled you since childhood. Your current upset is just a rehash of the one that has bothered you for a lifetime. You must dive deep inside yourself, shine the light on the false beliefs that have kept you small, and unveil the truth they are hiding. Jesus had no doubt about who he was, so the criticisms hurled at him did not deter him. When you know yourself as confidently as he did, disparaging words will have no power over you.

Waste no time defending, apologizing, or explaining yourself. Jesus did not debate with the naysayers. Their comments were not his business. His business was to speak and live the truth. He didn't spend energy trying to manage his impact. He simply moved on to initiate his ministry. The Jesus who forged ahead represents your authentic self stepping forth in dignity and confidence. You waste your energy engaging with people who do not understand you. Instead, give your attention to the affirmative voice. Just as Jesus emerged from the archaic temple unscathed, so will you.

The Real Inner Work

Many people do inner child work to get in touch with their innocent self. Others spend therapy time addressing their inner saboteur. How much more powerful would it be to do "inner Christ" work, in which you contact the part of you that is born of God, and bring that forth? Even while a part of you doubts, criticizes, or resists, another part is established in radiant wholeness. When you recognize your inherent divinity, all the other "inner" work falls into place beautifully.

The Torah that Jesus read from was not simply a parchment displaying printed words. It represents the book of our lives. As we unfurl it, the word of God is etched in our hearts. It promises us that we are loved and we will emerge unharmed from the dream of limitation and suffering. No more waiting, wishing, hoping, earning, or proving ourselves. In this day the scripture is fulfilled.

NEVER THIRST AGAIN

One day while traveling, Jesus grew tired and sat down by a well. Just then, a Samaritan woman came to draw water. Jesus told her, "Everyone who drinks the water you are drawing will be thirsty again. But whoever drinks the water I give them will never thirst again. The water I give them will become in them a spring welling up to eternal life."

The woman replied, "Sir, give me this water so I won't get thirsty and have to keep coming here to draw water."

He told her, "Go, call your husband and come back."

"I have no husband," she answered.

"That's right," Jesus replied. "You have had five husbands, and the man you are with now is not your husband."

Shocked, the woman replied, "Sir, I can see that you are a prophet . . . I know that the messiah called Christ is coming. When he comes, he will explain everything to us."

Then Jesus declared, "I, the one speaking to you—I am he."

The water the woman was drawing from the well symbolizes teachings or worldly pursuits that satisfy us for a moment, but soon we grow wanting again. Intellectual ideas and material quests fail to nourish the soul. A yogi once said, "Painted cakes cannot satisfy hunger." The teachings that Jesus and other great spiritual masters bring do not fade and lead us to more seeking. Instead, they grow richer and stronger as we put them into practice, and we no longer feel a need to reach outside ourselves for fulfillment. It's not enough to touch the world with our mind only. Ultimately we know life only through the heart.

Thirsty for Love

Jesus's encounter with this woman would have been incomplete without his inquiry about her many marriages. The woman was thirsty for love, attempting to satisfy her thirst through different men, without success. After each marriage, she grew more disappointed. If you can identify with her frustration, you can see that what appears to be a distant, ancient saga is really your own story.

The fulfillment the woman sought through external sources was available inside her. She already owned all the love she was reaching for through men, but she was looking for it in all the wrong places. If you, like her, feel exasperated in not finding true love through your relationships, job, or living situation, you are being redirected to the living waters within you.

Are You The One?

Many of us have spent a great deal of time and energy searching for "The One." We believe that destiny has designated for us one unique soulmate, and our task is to find him or her. Countless fairy tales, popular songs, romance novels, and movies have instilled and edified our belief in one partner who will offset our sense of deficiency and save us from loneliness. Then we set out on a long and frustrating journey of dating and marriage, kissing lots of frogs in our quest for Prince or Princess Charming. Behind our surface conversations, we silently wonder, "Are you The One?" When one person fails to fulfill our fantasy, we move on to the next date or marriage partner, asking even more fervently, "Are you The One?"

But it is not a person we are looking for. It is sense of wholeness. We fail to be satisfied by water drawn from a shallow well because there is a deeper well we thirst for. There is indeed One that will satisfy us, but it is not a person. It is a living spirit. This One is not limited to one body or personality. It is available everywhere, in all things that live. Its home is not another person, but your deep inner self. *The One is you.* You don't need another person to fulfill you. You carry The One within you. You have really been searching for yourself. When you fall—actually, rise—in love with yourself, you will find the profound soul reward you have been seeking elsewhere.

Winning the Real Lottery

I read an article by an accountant who studied the lives of lottery winners. While you might expect that winning the lottery would change people's lives for the better, in many cases their lives become more troubled. Some get into family fights over the windfall, others become alcoholic or depressed, and a few commit suicide. Most revert to their former level of wealth after a few years. I know a woman who won millions of dollars in a state lottery. Suddenly all kinds of friends, relatives, an ex-husband, and charities came out of the woodwork seeking a handout. She had to hire a bodyguard to accompany her six-year-old son throughout his days to avoid him being kidnapped. Receiving that huge sum was a mixed blessing.

Some lottery winners enjoy the money and use it to good advantage. Their lives are not ruined, but enhanced. After extensive analysis and interviews with the lottery winners, the accountant came to a simple conclusion: The people who were happy before they won the lottery were happy after they won the lottery. Those who were unhappy before winning, were unhappy after winning.

So it is with all of life. When we drink of living waters, our worldly walk becomes a blessing. We can have a soulmate or not, lots of money or not, a fancy home or not, a prestigious job or not. When we are fulfilled from the inside out, the external story is secondary. When we are connected with our spiritual Source, the right relationship, finances, health, home, and career follow naturally. Because the outer proceeds from the inner, as we line up with our soul, everything in the world configures in our favor.

Right in Front of You

When the woman at the well told Jesus that she was waiting for the messiah, she did not realize he was standing right in front of her. Likewise, the good that you seek may be available to you right where you are, but you might be missing it because you are looking elsewhere or waiting for it to come in the future.

My friend Larry spent many years searching for his soulmate. He had a long series of romantic relationships that didn't end up as he hoped. He would quickly fall in love and then, just as quickly, out. He confessed to me, "I spent more time partying and chasing illusions than connecting with quality women." All of his disappointments built up his heartfelt desire to share his life with a companion of character. More than ever, he felt, "I am ready."

Larry taught an evening class in English as a Second Language. In the next classroom, Sima taught a similar course. Larry thought Sima was attractive, but he didn't think about her as a relationship partner. For a year the two saw each other in the hallway and at faculty meetings. One evening after class they walked to their cars together and chatted in the parking lot. Since it was a cold night, Larry asked Sima if she wanted to continue their conversation over coffee. They went to a café and talked until it closed. The next week they went for coffee again, and Sima invited Larry for dinner at her apartment the following weekend. Before long the two were spending most of their time together. "One day it dawned on me that we were having a relationship without even trying," Larry told me with a chuckle. "I realized that Sima was a great woman down to her soul."

A year later, Larry and Sima were married. They have now been together over twenty years. When Larry met Sima, he had no idea she would become his life partner. Even while he was busy looking elsewhere, she was standing right in front of him.

Beyond a material manifestation, the spiritual reward you seek is available right where you stand. A Course in Miracles asks us to consider the people in our life, especially those we have a hard time with, and mentally request of them, "Give me your blessing, holy Son of God." In other words, "Let me behold the Christ in you." What Christ would not reveal himself to anyone who sincerely asks? When Jesus said, "Ask and it is given," he was referring partially to material rewards, but more fundamentally to spiritual awakening. You can get all the stuff you want, but, more importantly, you can find inner peace. Then you have it all.

Switch Tanks

At every moment we are choosing which well we will draw our sustenance from. Worldly water cannot satisfy our spiritual thirst. We eat a meal, and a few hours later we are hungry again. We go on a honeymoon, and soon we discover we are married to a real person rather than our fantasy. We land our ideal job, and then find things wrong with it. Nothing in form can satisfy our soul. We do not need to deny ourselves delicious food, a delightful honeymoon, or an exciting career. We need to quit denying ourselves the soul reward we have been missing.

I used to drive a truck that had two gas tanks. When one tank ran out of fuel, I pressed a button on the dashboard, and immediately the vehicle drew fuel from the other tank. A lot of us have run out of gas trying to import our good from people, things, and events. When our worldly supply becomes exhausted, we look elsewhere. As the outer world fails to satisfy us, we seek a higher answer. After enough frustrating relationships, jobs that almost work but don't, or houses in which we find cracks in the foundation, we look up. Then, in a flash, we find God standing right before us. At that moment our wait for the messiah is over, and we quench our spiritual thirst with living water after which we will never thirst again.

THE BEACON AND THE BASKET

I attended a seminar by Dr. Ihaleakala Hew Len, a lucid teacher of the ancient Hawaiian spiritual practice of *ho'opo-nopono*, or "healing through restoring balance." Dr. Hew Len lit a flashlight, pointed it toward the audience, and told us, "This light represents your true self." Then he held up a piece of glass and said, "This is your mind." He shined the flashlight through the glass and explained, "When your mind is clean and clear, your true self shines through brilliantly." Then he took a thick marker pen, covered the glass with black ink, and shined the flashlight through the glass again. This time the light that pierced the glass was quite dim. "When your mind is stained with fearful, limiting thoughts, your true self hardly shines through for the world to see." The teacher took a cloth, wiped the ink off the glass, and shined the light through it again, in full splendor. "Remove your dark thoughts, and your true self radiates as it was intended."

Jesus taught the same lesson in a metaphor of his time:

> You are the light of the world. People do not light a lamp and then put it under a bushel basket; it is set on a lampstand, where it gives light to all in the house. Likewise, your light must shine before others, that they may see your good deeds and glorify your heavenly Father.

The spiritual path is not about doing. It is about *undoing*, removing all that is not true and not you to reveal the glowing soul God created you to be. We were born fine, but then we got *de*fined. A truckload of burdensome definitions and labels were laid over us until but a spark of our innate divinity pierced though the mire. Now we are getting *re*fined, clearing away what is not God to reveal what *is* God, restoring the expression of our original nature.

Light Beyond the Body

The body is a window through which soul light shines. The form or condition of the body is not as important as the light emanating through it. Some people occupy bodies that are disabled or in some way limited. Yet their mind, heart, and soul are so clear and strong that the body fades to the background in the presence of the energy they are expressing.

A woman named Lori, confined to a wheelchair, attended one of my seminars. Lori had become paralyzed after a diving accident. She is one of the most radiant women I have ever seen.

The moment Lori entered the meeting room, she lit it up with her smile and her glowing presence. She celebrated all of her interactions with her fellow participants, and hugged generously. Lori was living in a heavenly state of mind, and she invited everyone she met to join here there. Her body's restrictions could not stop Lori's inner light from blessing everyone she encountered.

Some people may take on physical limitations to demonstrate to others that the condition of the body cannot dampen our spirit. *A Course in Miracles* asks us to remember, "I am not a body. I am free. I am as God created me." Most of us are so identified with our body that what happens to our body, happens to our mind. The body feels good, and we are happy. The body has a pain or we experience some kind of restriction, as minimal as sitting in a traffic jam, and we become upset. Yet the body rules our happiness only when we attribute power to it. We all have the power to maintain our identity as luminous beings independent of what our body or other material circumstances are doing. We are the beacon, not the basket.

Where the Light Comes From

You may have practiced meditations in which you absorb light and healing from an external source, such as the sun or a spiritual master. While these meditations have practical value, there is a slight distortion in the dynamic. While we seem to be importing light from an external source, we are really *emanating* light from an internal source. Absorbing energy from somewhere out there is a permission slip by which we use an object as a focal point to achieve our desired result. Ultimately *there is no outside source*. There is not even an inside source separate from ourselves. We *are* the source we seem to be drawing energy from. Jesus did not say, "Get the light of the world." He said, "You *are* the light of the world." He identified us with the good we seek. We carry light with us wherever we go because we carry ourselves wherever we go. You cannot be separate from what you are. In this realization is the great homecoming. You cannot simultaneously be a limited body and limitless light. The moment comes when we shift our identity from the frail to the majestic, from the fleeting to the eternal.

Everything You Need to Heal

The world by itself has no meaning, power, or purpose. It is simply the stage upon which we play out our journey of awakening. Only when we add the light of higher awareness to our earthly existence does our life make sense. Our divine nature animates and ennobles all that we do. Every soul is holy because we have the capacity to light the world. When we do, we fulfill our purpose and our heart is at peace.

Modern medical technology corroborates Jesus's teaching by using light to heal. Physicians and veterinarians use laser light machines to rejuvenate damaged and diseased organs. Dentists harden tooth fillings with a blue light. Urologists focus a green laser light to reduce the size of enlarged prostates. Phototherapy treatments alleviate mood, sleep, and skin disorders, psoriasis, eczema, and acne. Hospitals sanitize instruments with UV light, cutting infection rates. Light is not just a tool of medicine. Light *is* medicine.

All technology replicates spiritual faculties we embody, but have atrophied because we do not use them. We can accomplish all that machines accomplish by the intelligent application of mind. Jesus achieved all the healings that modern machines achieve, and more, without any device, and so can we. Everything you need to heal yourself and others already lives within you. When we have the faith in our mind that we have in technology, we will move ahead at light speed. Our mind is the greatest technological instrument ever bestowed upon us by God.

Give Your Gift

More than anything, the universe loves to see your true self shine. When you are happy, you bless everyone you meet. You affect the world more by your energy than your actions. If you do good deeds but your spirit is dampened, your deed is not so good. When you are delighted, you are a healer. Some parents worry about their children growing up with negative or fearful attitudes. I advise them to teach their children joy by example. When you live your most passionate life, you serve as a role model of well-being and you inspire your children to do the same. If you model self-care, authentic expression, and a prosperous mindset, your children will learn from your example. They will find their perfect niche in the great scheme of things, and be successful as well as happy. Then your heart will be at peace, knowing that you guided your children to live a joy-filled life.

The world is starving for light. Those who bring it are the deliverers of humanity. Never underestimate the gift you bring when you let your true self shine. Shift your focus from the form of what you are doing to the energy behind your actions. Your light has not been dampened in the least by any basket covering it; it is the one flame the world cannot extinguish. You don't have to become the light of the world. That is what you already are. Now all that is left is for you to let the world bask in your divine radiance.

HEALING
ALLOWED

During a residential program I was leading at a spiritual retreat center, I was having lunch with several participants at an outdoor picnic table. One student rose, stood behind me, and kindly began to massage my neck and shoulders. I sat with my eyes closed, savoring the thoughtful touch.

Suddenly I was jarred by a deep voice booming, "Healing is not allowed here!" Certain this was another student playing a prank, I opened my eyes to see who it was. To my surprise, the retreat center security guard was standing behind us. He looked the part: burly, a close-shorn crew cut, gut brimming over his belt. I read the name on his badge: George. I looked at the man in disbelief.

"No healing is allowed on the campus except in the healing temple," the guard bellowed. "If you want to be healed, you have to go there."

My friends and I cracked up. This had to be a joke. Who would make a rule against someone being healed? I looked again at George and saw that he was dead serious. The student removed her hands from my shoulders and sat down. The guard, satisfied he had done his job, nodded and moved on.

After lunch, as I was walking back to my room, I saw George heading my way. More relaxed now, I figured this would be a good chance to have some fun with him. "Sorry about that healing back there," I told him. "I don't know what came over me."

The guard shot me a stern look. "I hope you understand. If I let you do healing there, before you know it, people will be healing all over the place!"

I had to muster all the will power I could to keep a straight face. I nodded and told George, "And that's the last thing we would want to happen, isn't it?"

"That's right," he replied staunchly, and marched on his way.

I dashed to my room, closed the door behind me, and roared with laughter. This was too weird to be true. Then I flashed on a Bible story that reminded me of the incident:

On a Sabbath day, Jesus was teaching in a synagogue when a woman who had been crippled for eighteen years pleaded with him to heal her. Jesus called her forth and told her, "Woman, you are set free from your infirmity." He placed his hands on her, and immediately she straightened up and thanked God.

The temple leader, observing this feat, was outraged. "The rules of the religion prohibit healing on the Sabbath!" he rebuked Jesus.

"You hypocrites!" Jesus retorted. "Don't you on the Sabbath day untie your ox or donkey and take it to water? Why, then, should this woman who has been bound for eighteen years not be set free?"

Jesus was criticized for breaking many rules of the Jewish religion. He forgave adulterers and prostitutes, fraternized with Romans and tax collectors, overturned the prescribed diet, and drove merchants out of the great temple. He laid into the religious leaders for being small-minded and two-faced. No wonder he was crucified. He defied the letter of the law in order to honor the spirit of the law. The apostle Paul said, "the letter kills, but the spirit gives life."

Every religion began with an inspired prophet who had a striking revelation and helped people come closer to God. Every religion has also become ensnared in the trappings of dogma. When truth is institutionalized, it becomes a breeding ground for fear-based control, which stifles the flame of love the religion was intended to fan. Only when we pierce to the pure source of the religion, the brilliant insight that preceded its impediments, do we attain the blessings the religion was intended to deliver.

Jesus deftly illuminated the difference between the spirit of the law and the letter of the law when he explained, "The sabbath was made for man, not man for the sabbath."

Where Healing Takes Place

Ironically, George the security guard was upholding a metaphysical principle that had become confused with a physical location. It is true that healing can take place only in the healing temple. But the healing temple is not a physical building. It is a state of mind. You and I carry the healing temple within us wherever we go. We access it by elevating our consciousness. When we step back from our mundane activities and look up, all the benefits of healing accrue to us.

God does not need a police force to uphold the truth. Universal principles are self-evident, self-policing, and work at all times in all places and circumstances. When we confuse physical structures with the purpose they represent, we lose sight of the source of our healing. Because we are fundamentally mental and spiritual beings, it is what our mind and spirit are doing that determines the quality of our life. You are allowed and invited to be healed any time, at any place. God does not live in a building. God lives in your heart.

Rules or Laws?

The mystical messiah showed us how to discern between God-made laws and human-made rules. Some human rules match God's laws, and many don't. Rules that people make are generally fear-based, and God's laws are founded in love. God's will is compassion, not vengeance. When we give grace, we are most Godlike. Every day offers us many opportunities to practice giving grace, and also to receive it.

I once had to change an airplane flight at the last minute. As I approached the airline counter at the airport, I worried that I would be charged a stiff change-of-flight fee and increased fare. I showed my ticket to the agent, a short Black bald-headed man with wire-rimmed glasses. He studied my ticket and then scanned his computer. "It says here I'm supposed to charge you an extra $400 to get on the flight this morning," he began. "But my reading skills are rather poor, so I didn't see that. Here's your boarding pass. Have a nice flight."

After thanking the fellow, I walked away thinking that I might do well to unsharpen some of *my* reading skills. Too often I have been tempted to hold people to rules rather than extend mercy. To the human mind, "the law" is a frightening word because most of humanity's laws are based on punishment. To the divine mind, "the law"—God's law—is a cause for joy and celebration. To be a "God-fearing" person is an oxymoron. Anyone who fears God does not know God. Why would you fear someone who gave you life, sustains you, loves you infinitely and eternally, and wants only the best for you?

Healing the Inner Pharisees

As gentle as Jesus was with people who had been condemned, he was tough with the condemners. "You blind guides!" he chastised the Pharisees. "You strain your water so you won't accidentally swallow a gnat, but you swallow a camel!" He was calling these leaders out for becoming so immersed in petty rules that they lost sight of love. They had become spiritually penny wise and dollar foolish. He sought to correct their vision so they would help people rather than judge them.

The Pharisees are not simply dark-cloaked figures spewing dogma from the murky halls of an ancient religion. To this day, inner Pharisees maintain an outpost in your head and mine. A part of our mind is absorbed in smallness, hiding in a maze of details, addicted to control, succumbed to the tyranny of the trivial. *A Course in Miracles* urges us to rise above "the thunder of the meaningless." Let us not allow minutia to dominate our consciousness and decimate our joy.

Any time we get hung up on details at the expense of the big picture, we reenact the Pharisees' obsession with rules over life. When we make healing our priority, we free ourselves and others. My friends Mark and his wife Marcia are avid religious Jews. When their son Joel decided to marry a Native American woman, Mark and Marcia were initially upset by their son's choice. Joel's fiancée was nice enough, but she didn't match their vision of who their son should marry and how the wedding ceremony should be conducted. After an unpleasant round of angst and arguments, Mark and Marcia decided that their goal was for their son to be happy even if his choice of a marriage partner was not theirs for him. So they quit fighting his decision and they supported the couple to have the wedding they valued, which included Jewish elements and Native American rituals. Since the fiancée's parents didn't have much money, Mark and Marcia paid for the affair. They decided to go beyond the letter of the law to live the spirit of the law. Now their hearts are at peace, their son and his wife feel loved, and the family gatherings are filled with harmony.

Grace in Action

We can join Jesus as a grace giver, right where we stand. At a recent graduation ceremony of Morehouse College, one of the largest institutions of higher learning for African American students, corporate magnate Robert F. Smith delivered the commencement address. Smith stunned the student body by announcing that he would pay off the student loans of every graduating senior. With about four hundred seniors, each averaging a hundred thousand dollars in student debt, Smith's generous gift amounted to about four million dollars.

Can you imagine the joy and release those seniors felt when they found out they wouldn't have to work for years to pay off their student loans? This exhilarating experience represents the deep inner peace we enjoy when we realize that God has forgiven our karmic debts. How liberated would you feel to know that all forms of owingness that you experience have just been wiped out?

You don't have to be a millionaire to give grace. When someone feels guilty for rescheduling a meeting with you, you can simply say, "Not a problem." Or if they apologize for showing up late, tell them, "This was a good chance for me to reply to a few texts." Or if your child doesn't get all A's on his report card, compliment him on the good grades he did get. Each day offers us many opportunities to extend grace.

Let's not stop with giving others grace. We must accept grace for ourselves, as well. You may feel overwhelmed by a gnawing sense of obligation, the feeling that "there is so much more I have to do before I can relax." Eventually your "to do" list becomes an unbearable load. While ego tells you how burdened you are, grace takes the pack off your back. Grace reminds you that you always have enough time and resources to do what you need to do. God is not pressuring you. You are pressuring yourself. You don't have to jump lots of spiritual hurdles before you can cross the finish line. In the eyes of God, you've already crossed the finish line. Miracles, which we all deserve, wipe out karma. Jesus came to demonstrate that we are not sinful, God is not wrathful, and we do not owe.

All such oppressive interpretations of ourselves and God are the products of a mistaken mind. When we purify our mind by seeing ourselves and each other through the eyes of love, we purge the inner Pharisees and restore ourselves to our worthy place in the cosmos.

Every day presents us with many choices between gnats and camels, littleness and magnitude, details and glory, lack and supply, humanity's limits and God's freedom. Jesus was allowed to heal on the Sabbath because it was his Father's will, and you are likewise allowed to do what Spirit calls you to do. If you are not sure whether to do something, ask yourself if it is spiritually legal. Is this act in alignment with your sense of integrity and living true to your Source? Is it adding more light and happiness to your life or the life of someone you touch? The Christ in you is stepping forward to purge your mind and life of all oppression. Healing is not only allowed, but necessary. At some point, you find the courage to do what you are here to do. Let no fear-based rule stand between you and the life you came to live.

THE SINGLE EYE

My friend Colleen was diagnosed with cancer of the tongue. After several months of attempting treatment with drugs, her doctor informed her that he would have to surgically remove her tongue. This dismal prospect motivated Colleen to join a Christian healing group. There the leader asked her to stand in the middle of a circle of people and receive a healing prayer from the group. When Colleen closed her eyes, she saw what appeared to be a bolt of lightning enter her mouth and strike where the cancer was located. Afterward, she felt a deep peace.

A few days later, Colleen went for pre-op x-rays, and the doctor was shocked. There was no trace of any cancer. She was entirely healed. That experience occurred thirty-two years ago. Since that time, Colleen has enjoyed excellent health.

As a result of her spiritual healing, Colleen has developed a close connection with Jesus Christ and the Blessed

Mother. She has an avid prayer life and has made pilgrimages to the sacred sites of Lourdes, Assisi, and Medjugorje. She has become a hospice volunteer, cancer care counselor, and holistic life coach. While the experience was initially harrowing, Colleen recognizes that the process guided her to her true spiritual path.

The master lightworker Jesus taught,

> The eye is the lamp of the body. If your eye be single,
> your body will be filled with light. If your eye is not
> sound, your whole body shall be filled with darkness.

The "single eye" Jesus refers to is spiritual vision, which recognizes only wholeness and perfection. This higher way of seeing knows that we are beings of pure energy. Jesus was so established in his vision of perfection that the people he was called to heal rose to that consciousness with him, and they were made whole. In truth, they were always whole. But they were temporarily distracted by double vision, the world of duality and polarity that forms the matrix of the physical universe.

A healer, counselor, or teacher is a visionary. He or she uses a higher way of seeing than the one to which the world subscribes. If you go into agreement that there are two powers, rather than one, you open up Pandora's box of a world of conflict, oppression and victimization, a devil with the ability to oppose and triumph over God, and all the pain and sorrow that characterize humanity. While the world of duality seems real when you are in it, including all the hardships it generates, in the greater picture it cannot tear the fabric of wholeness upon which reality is established.

If Jesus were to walk the world today, he would use modern metaphors and parables to transmit his lessons. He might say, "If you wish to listen to the radio station that plays your favorite music, you must keep your tuner set on that frequency. If you change frequency, you will lose your valued signal." Genius scientist Nikola Tesla underscored the same principle: "If you want to find the secrets of the universe, think in terms of energy, frequency and vibration." Healing occurs at one frequency, disease at another. To give or receive healing, you must keep your tuner fixed on the higher vibration.

> No servant can serve two masters, for either he
> will hate the one and love the other, or he will be
> devoted to the one and despise the other.

You cannot live in two worlds at once. You cannot simultaneously fear and love; be in integrity and duplicity; cavort in illusions and remember the truth; be a physical body and know yourself as an eternal spirit. You cannot say you believe in God and complain about the devil. Every moment offers a choice of the consciousness we will live in. "In my Father's mansion there are many rooms" means that we live in a universe of multiple simultaneous realities, and we inhabit the one that matches the thoughts we hold. A split mind sees a fragmented universe. A single mind sees unified creation. You may not have a choice about all the realities out there, but you do have a choice about which one you will dwell in. Neither can you control the realities that other people choose to dwell in. You must respect the right of others to choose their reality, while respecting your right to choose yours.

Which Picture Do You See?

In the inspiring movie *Resurrection*, Ellen Burstyn portrays Edna Mae, a woman who discovers she has the power to heal. She then goes about helping many people. One day a crippled young man comes to her, and she restores him. A doctor who observed the healing tells Edna Mae, "But I saw the pictures" (referring to the x-rays). Edna Mae smiles and tells him, "I didn't see those pictures," meaning that she was seeing the patient through a higher vision than the one the x-rays revealed.

A healer sees past the appearance of illness, into the reality of wellness. When you replace "i" with "we," "illness" becomes "wellness." Disease is a result of a mind that sees separation from God. Wellness knows we are one with God. Some doctors are also healers. While they are offering medical treatment, they simultaneously hold the vision of the patient's perfect higher self. If you are such a doctor, or you find your way to one, you are blessed indeed. Such high-minded treatment maximizes the patient's opportunity for total healing.

The mystical messiah emphasized the importance of single vision many times. He said, "Choose this day whom you will serve." In other words, "Decide which vision you will use." When the disciple Peter asked Jesus, "What about him?" referring to Judas, who would later betray Jesus, the master answered, "What is that to you? Just follow me." He was telling Peter not to focus on opposition, but to keep his vision trained on the goal. People who battle darkness magnify darkness. People who are immersed in good expand good. Attention is an investment in more of the same. If you want to live in the kingdom of heaven, you must focus on it exclusively.

Do You Trust Him, or Don't You?

When I needed some intricate dental work, I did some research and found a dentist I believed could do the job. This dental process required a series of steps, some costly. As we began treatment, I wondered if the dentist was advising me accurately and charging me fairly. He did a good job on the first step, and when he got to the second step, I was tempted to question him. Then a voice in my head asked me, "Do you trust him, or don't you?" If I was going to trust this man, I had to trust him totally. It would do me no good to doubt and test him at every turn. If he was worthy of my trust, he was trustworthy in all aspects. Since I am not a dentist, I had to turn the whole project over to him, not just parts. Ultimately he did an excellent job, and my trust in him was justified.

If we are going to trust God, we must trust God entirely, not just in selected areas of our life. We cannot say, "I believe you will take care of my health, but as for my relationship . . . well, that's a different story." Either God is in charge of the universe, or God is not. Either God is everywhere, or God is nowhere. The idea of a partial God is meaningless. There are no spaces that God has left vacant. We must adopt the innocent trust of a little child who depends on her parents to nurture and protect her. "To enter the kingdom of heaven, you must become like a little child."

Don't Split Your Power

In a *Superman* television episode, the caped crusader goes to South America to help the leader of a country threatened by revolutionaries. There Superman is arrested and jailed. But he must escape to help the leader avoid assassination, while maintaining the appearance of being in jail. So Superman attempts the dangerous feat of splitting himself into two entities. But then he risks weakening himself and losing his superpowers, or, even worse, he may not be able to reintegrate his divided selves.

When we split ourselves off from our Christed identity, we divide our mind into the belief in two selves, one godly and one mortal. Then we dilute our strength. To maintain our authentic power, we must be one mind and one self. Like Superman, we must reunite our fragmented selves to regain our superpowers. After years or lifetimes of being fractured and worn down by dualistic existence, we may become depressed, disheartened, or sick. We might feel like we are in a psychic jail. Yet the descent into duality motivates us to find our way back to one self. Superman eventually discovered how to get himself back together, and so will we. Sooner or later, we exchange our two selves for one.

Uniting the Kingdom

A Pharisee who was an expert in religious law tried to test Jesus: "What is the greatest commandment in Judaism?" Jesus answered, "Love God with all your heart and all your soul and all your mind." The mystical messiah was urging us to keep our single eye on the benevolent universe. Einstein stated, "I think the most important question facing humanity is, 'Is the universe a friendly place?'" Jesus answered that question long before Einstein posed it. Each of us must come to that profound insight through our own inquiry. We must decide whether we will see a universe divided against itself, or a universe unified by one Creator with one Mind. When we use the mind that Jesus used, we see as God sees, we know as God knows, and we are healed as God is perfect.

In the movie *The Dark Crystal*, a kingdom has become split into two drastically opposite factions: The gentle Mystics and the evil Skeksis. The Mystics are kindly but powerless, and the Skeksis are powerful but selfish. Their predicament is symbolized by a huge crystal that has become shattered, the remnants scattered in different places throughout the kingdom. The movie's hero Jen is given the task of reuniting the severed pieces of the crystal. A seer charges Jen to fulfill an ancient prophecy that what was torn apart and undone shall be whole, and the two made one. When Jen replaces the broken shard, the Mystics and Skeksis come together and create a new race of unspeakable glory. Their original magnificence is restored. The climax of this movie is one of the most stunning metaphysical images of all cinema, highly recommended and well worth watching for the entire family.

Dedicated to the One Eye, Love

While illness, pain, and death are strong appearances in the world of illusion, in truth they have no power or reality. All sorrow is the progeny of separation, and all healing proceeds from unity. Christians call Satan "the liar." When you regard someone as sick, broken, or limited, you are reinforcing their pain by boxing them into an identity smaller than befits them. When you see them as complete and radiant, you open the door to their freedom. The higher the vision you hold of your dear ones, the more likely they are to step into it. Jesus healed the sick and raised the dead because he did not see them as sick or dead. He saw only the wholeness of their spirit. His vision of their well-being was so strong that he jump-started their vision, like a fully-charged car battery stimulates an apparently dead battery to come back to life. While we may turn our back on life, life will never turn its back on us, because life is what we are. You can dream you have departed from your true Self, but you cannot achieve that impossible situation. This is the fail-safe that God has imbued in His beloved children.

The most sacred prayer in Judaism is "Hear O Israel, the Lord our God is One." This is more of a metaphysical affirmation than a prayer. The universe is holographic. Everything is connected to everything. There is One Mind, not many. When we see the unity behind the appearance of separation, we are seeing as Jesus saw, and our single eye reveals that we have not traveled a distance from God, but we have been home all along.

BLESSED ARE

My friend Regina went through a painful divorce that rocked her world. When she had married Brad, Regina thought for sure they would be together forever. That happy vision was cut short when, after ten years, Brad informed her that he was leaving her. "I didn't see that one coming," she told me. "But, thinking back, I realized that the love we once shared was no longer there. Over the years we had drifted farther and farther apart. Our communication had dwindled to a mere trickle. What started out as a love story had degenerated to an empty shell."

"Then what happened?" I had to ask.

"While the divorce was heartbreaking, I began to reclaim my power and reassemble the shattered elements of myself. I joined a progressive church, went to yoga class, and developed my interior design business. I came alive for the first time in a long time. Some physical issues I had been dealing with cleared up. The weight I had put on to protect myself during my marriage melted away. After a year I met James, and we began a healthy relationship that now lights my world. What started out as the most painful experience opened the door to a new and far more rewarding life."

While divorces and other life stressors are painful, they often lead to awakening, healing, and transformation we would not have achieved in an easier situation. The hardship cannot erase the blessings we once enjoyed, and we find hidden gifts in the experience. While the personality moves through a difficult process, the soul is emerging. What seemed to be a setback turns out to be a setup for something better.

In the famous Sermon on the Mount, Jesus explained how blessed we all are, even when it doesn't appear to be so. The mystical messiah invited us to claim grace. This sacred state transforms stumbling blocks into stepping stones, and upgrades our vision of people we observe who seem downtrodden, victimized, and marginalized. In that stirring address, Jesus delivered solace to the sick, reprieve to the guilty, courage to the fearful, and hope to all who yearn to be freed from suffering.

The Mountaintop Viewpoint

Jesus's ascent to a lofty elevation represents the Christed part of our mind that views life from a higher level of consciousness. This voice imparts truth we cannot hear when we are immersed in ground-level activities. The audience who met Christ at altitude indicates that the human mind is capable of rising beyond the mundane to connect with our higher self and absorb its wisdom.

In setting forth the beatitudes, the mystical messiah was not simply promising future redemption or consoling sorrowful people with the hope that one day their plight would be vindicated. Jesus was underscoring the *alreadyness* of salvation. These were *be*-attitudes, not *becoming*-attitudes; here-and-now blessings rather than "we'll get there someday." The master did not say, "Blessed will be." He said, "Blessed *are*."

Join me now as we sit before the master as he sets forth the truths that yield the healing we yearn for:

**Blessed are the poor in spirit,
for theirs is the kingdom of heaven.**

The poor in spirit own the kingdom of heaven because they carry it within them. While the personality may feel poor, the soul is eternally rich. The human self may feel daunted, but the divine self remains fully empowered. It is tempting to go up and down with the wins and losses of daily life. Finances, relationships, or health issues may drag us down. But the peaks and valleys of worldly experience cannot mar our divine legacy. Be not distracted by the changing appearances of the world. Your true self is established in perfect well-being even while your human self moves through changes. Love remains real even when fear seems to rule. At any moment we can return our mind to blessings, which far outshine any sense of lack that may tempt us.

**Blessed are those who mourn,
for they will be comforted.**

Mourners shall be comforted because one day they will understand that no one really dies. Everyone who seems to die remains with us. What lives cannot die and what dies cannot live. One day you will be reunited with everyone who has gone on—and a glorious reunion it shall be! In the world of time, those who grieve shall eventually find peace. In the world beyond time, mourners may take comfort now because the love they believe they have lost is still very much with them. The spirit does not weep because, being life, it knows only life. Only the ego perceives loss and death. Meanwhile the deepest, truest part of ourself recognizes that life is eternal, and no appearance can sever us from the presence of love.

Blessed are the meek,
for they will inherit the Earth.

"Meek" means "humble." While arrogant people fight over money, territory, possessions, and power, the humble do not participate in ego-based conflicts. They quietly go about their business whilst warmongers cancel each other out. Healer Bruno Gröning said, "Evil gets caught in its own nets." While fighters go down, lovers thrive.

The part of you that is relaxed, trusting, and not seduced by fear will emerge triumphant. When the ego has exhausted its self-defeating campaigns, your spirit will prevail. As we realize we are the offspring of the Most High, the splendor, beauty, and majesty of the physical universe are at our behest for our appreciation and enjoyment.

Blessed are those who hunger and thirst for
righteousness, for they will be filled.

Amidst the illusions that keep the world spinning in agony, the children of God seek to know and live a higher reality. Spiritual beings value integrity more than compromise. Seekers of truth are already filled because their noble values elevate them above the fray.

The story of the world implies that the good are downtrodden and evil people triumph. The media are filled with accounts of war, murder, cruelty, and corruption. Watching the news is depressing because the news is immersed in illusions, not truth. Yet there is a different kind of news that brings upliftment. When you withdraw your attention from reports based on fear, titillation, and sensationalism, you reclaim the serenity those reports shredded.

Social injustice cannot offset divine justice, which is founded in forgiveness, not punishment. While fright feverishly rattles its sabers, love quietly trusts. When terror has exhausted its last "huff and puff to blow your house down," the house of God stands gleaming in the sun. Evil is a bad movie we don't need to continue to watch. At any moment we are free to exit the theater and inhale the fresh air of a benevolent universe.

One day evil movies will fade to their native nothingness, and the original movie God intended will replace them. We have the capacity to enter that theater now if we are willing to focus on the world we prefer rather than the one we fear.

Blessed are the merciful,
for they will be shown mercy.

The thoughts and feelings you hold about others pass through you at the moment you generate them. When you love someone, you are uplifted by the love you give. If you judge, berate, or hate someone, you instantly experience the dark effects of those psychic choices. You receive what you give, as you give it. Where mind goes, experience follows.

The merciful, steeped in the mindset of helpfulness, do not expect to be punished by God, and they do not punish themselves. Vengeance and forgiveness function in two entirely different realities; to affirm one is to deny the other.

When you extend mercy to others, mercy befalls you instantly. Jesus's promises refer not just to the return of good karma in the future, but the experience of good karma at the moment it is offered. When you are absorbed in kindness, there is no room for any other experience. To give mercy is to become one with a God of mercy, and awaken from the nightmare of sin and punishment.

Blessed are the pure in heart,
for they will see God.

The world we see depends on the vision we are using to see it. The lenses of love and fear reveal entirely different landscapes. If we are consumed with anger, resentment, guilt, revenge, or material pursuits, our vision of God is obscured. What we see represents a choice; we find the world we are looking for. A pure heart seeks and finds only well-being. When we cleanse our vision, the God we seek appears before us. That God has always been with us, but we did not see Him or Her because we were looking elsewhere. A pure heart finds ever-present love.

Blessed are the peacemakers,
for they will be called children of God.

War is not the will of God. It is engendered by people who feel separated from love. While war occurs between people and nations, it more fundamentally occurs *within* people. A split mind generates a split world. Outer peace is impossible as long as there is inner turmoil. Peace of soul is the forerunner of peace on Earth. *A Course in Miracles* asks, "Can the world be saved if you are not?"

A healthy mind does not accept war as a fact of life. What is not of peace is not of God. Conflict is hell because it is divorced from reality. Many religions have waged war, ravaged, and killed in the name of God. No greater falsehood has ever been perpetrated. God unites people and integrates the elements within each person. God is wholeness, never brokenness or separation. The children of God enjoy completion now, and lead the world to peace by modeling it.

Blessed are they who are persecuted
for the sake of righteousness,
for theirs is the kingdom of heaven.

Criticism and persecution cannot diminish your true self. Unjust attack edifies your self-knowledge, as it drives you inward to find the noblest truth about yourself and hold firmly to it. People who make a stand for a greater reality are threatening to those steeped in fear. Yet at some point we find no alternative to authenticity. When the values you have been taught by the world grow empty, you establish your life on higher ground.

Let us not misinterpret Jesus's statement to glorify martyrdom. He was not calling us to seek persecution or carry the old rugged cross. To the contrary, he was calling us to lay down the cross and walk tall as whole persons. Jesus does not want us to adopt a victim mentality. If you are at peace with yourself and

God, external attacks are powerless. You are in heaven because you occupy your right mind.

As God Thinks

When the disciple Peter expressed his doubts to Jesus, the master told him, "Peter, you are thinking as people think, not as God thinks." The beatitudes are statements of how God thinks. When we feel poor, downtrodden, or persecuted, we have forgotten our inherent abundance, empowerment, and right to divine justice. At such a moment we need to lift our vision and recognize that in the spiritual dimension there is no lack, loss, or victimization. Jesus was teaching us to pierce beyond the veil of appearances and see into reality.

Christ's stunning words on the mountainside have traveled across the centuries like flaming arrows to pierce our hearts and open them to recognize the gifts laid at our door. Now you know what he knows. Now you feel what he feels. Now you are what he is. That glorious awakening is precisely what the mystical messiah came to accomplish. Now it is done.

THE PRODIGAL'S GIFT

The prodigal son is the most famous of Jesus's parables for good reason. In this brief yet epic tale, Jesus illuminates the entire dynamic of humanity's self-imposed separation from God, and—even more important—our momentous return. If this were the only teaching Christ delivered during his sojourn on Earth, his contribution would remain paramount.

A certain man had two sons. The younger one demanded of his father, "Give me my inheritance now." The son took his wealth and traveled to a far country, where he fell in with bad company and squandered his fortune on riotous living. When he had exhausted his funds, a great famine fell over the land, and he began to starve.

So he took a job with a man who sent him to feed his pigs. The son became so hungry that the slop the pigs ate began to look good to him. But still, no one fed him.

The young man's suffering led him to realize what a fool he had been. He considered that his father's servants had plenty of food, while he was starving. He said, "I will go home and apologize to my father and God. I will tell him I am no longer worthy to be called his son, and I will ask him to hire me as a servant."

As the fellow approached his home, still a distance off, his father saw him. The elder was filled with compassion, and ran and embraced the boy. The son told his father of his foolishness and his unworthiness to be his son. But the father was so glad to have his son come back that he told his servants to dress him in fine clothing and put a ring on his finger. The happy father made a great feast, where all were merry.

The elder son, hearing the festivities, refused to attend. He told his father, "I have served you for so many years, followed all of your rules, and I never disobeyed you. But you never made a feast for me and my friends. Now this other son is back, after wasting your money on prostitutes, and you made a huge party for him."

His father said, "Son, you are always with me, and everything I have is yours. It is right that we should celebrate and be happy, for your brother was dead to us and is alive again; he was lost and is found."

As children of God, we are all heir to the gifts of the kingdom. We were born brimming with life force and the power to create. Still connected to heaven, we dwelt in a state of pure joy and we lighted the lives of those who looked upon us.

Then we got involved in a world that distracted us from our ecstatic nature. We made choices that depleted our vibrant energy rather than enhancing it. We sank into judgment, divisiveness, negative self-talk, and guilt, and we adopted a demeaning self-image. We gave our attention to discouraging news, gossip, fault-finding, mass panic, and warfare. We mistreated our bodies, got trapped in addictions, and lost ourselves in amassing possessions, seeking social status, and climbing the corporate ladder. We became hypnotized with technology, overwork, and worry. We squandered the gifts of God rather than investing them in uplifting activities that brought us authentic joy.

Eventually "a famine fell over the land," and the goals we thought would make us happy bottomed out. The people we sought to please ignored or turned against us; the marriage we thought would complete us left us feeling empty and alone; our corporate striving yielded anxiety and ulcers; a market crash decimated our holdings; the religion that promised us heaven, deposited us in hell; the technology we thought would make our lives easier, made us crazy; and the worry we thought would protect us left us more insecure than ever. We were starving for peace and healing.

Every soul reaches a turning point where we realize that we have been living in a very foreign land indeed, and we just want to go home. And a magnificent vision that is! We realize that the values we have adopted were never our own. Now all we want is to be happy, and we will do whatever that takes. We reverse direction and head toward our Father's house, seeking to reclaim the gifts of Spirit instead of the hollow rewards of the world.

Yet even as we prepare our apology speech to God, we are interrupted by His loving voice, bidding us, "Welcome home, my beloved child. No apology is necessary. All I care about is that you are with me again." This occasion is surely worthy of a great feast! You were among the walking dead, and now you have come back to life.

Above all, Jesus Christ was a teacher of grace. He took away the sins of the world by demonstrating that none of our sins were so great that they could cause us to lose the love of our heavenly Father. God is not interested in punishing us. Even while we mete out self-punishment, God wants only to embrace us. The long, hard journey through a land of suffering is over. We are on our way home.

The Righteous Brother

Meanwhile, the elder brother is jealous because he did all that he was asked, and his father never threw him the festive party his younger brother now enjoys. A bit of history will illuminate Jesus's reason for adding this postscript to the story. His audience was comprised of Jewish people living under the onus of a multitude of laws they had to obey. Orthodox Judaism prescribes six hundred and thirteen detailed commandments that every pious Jew must meticulously fulfill. Religious people sweated to execute the letter of the law so they would be considered righteous in the eyes of God and the community. To the extent that they were sincere, they achieved the blessings a religious life bestows.

Jesus's ministry was directed toward people who were suffering more intensely, hungry to be healed. He reached out to people who were discouraged and disheartened, and yearned to be released from their sorrow. As a result, he was severely criticized by the Jews for fraternizing with sinners. So he delivered the addendum to the parable to help religious people understand the importance of extricating people who had gotten lost in a world of pain.

Jesus was diplomatically validating religious practitioners for their good works and their efforts to be close to God. Their devotion had helped them escape the trappings of an out-of-control life. They remained in the Father's house all the while. Thus he embraced the pious as well as the penitent. The mystical messiah covered all of his bases in this cathartic parable.

Welcoming the Inner Prodigal

As in all of Jesus's parables, there is a deeper intrapersonal meaning. We all have an element in our mind that believes we must follow religious or societal rules to earn the love of God or gain social respect. We may live a disciplined life that works for us. We also have an inner prodigal who is prone to some form of riotous living. These two elements seem to be at war with each other, constantly vying for our attention and expression. We all know the angel on one shoulder urging us to do the right thing, and the devil on the other shoulder prodding us to do the fun thing. Both of these tendencies play out in our lives.

The righteous son appears to be closer to God because he is following all the rules. But, truth be told, he is less than fulfilled because much of his life is about duty; he is largely motivated by fear of being punished if he does not toe the line. Yet he avoids the kind of messes that the prodigal son gets involved in. His life is more peaceful, but less passionate.

The prodigal, on the other hand, is on the express route to awakening. He is a practitioner of tantric yoga, immersed in the activities of the world to learn their results. He is amassing more pain, but when he is fed up with his poor choices, his illumination is profound and lasting.

Which of the sons dwells foremost within you? Do you follow the rules, but wish you had more fun? Do you let your party self rip, bang your head against a wall, and then course correct? What are the benefits of the path you have chosen? What are its debits? How has your route fostered your spiritual awakening?

Let the Weeds Grow

The story of the prodigal son parallels Jesus's other parable in which a farmer plants wheat seeds, but an enemy infiltrates the field and plants weeds. When the farmer's servants ask him if he wants them to pull out the weeds, he answers, "No, because then you will uproot the good plants along with the bad. Wait until the wheat and the weeds have both grown, and then throw the weeds away and place the wheat in the barn."

Sometimes it is beneficial for bad habits to develop side by side with good habits, so when they are both mature, the contrast between them is obvious. Then we become very clear which we prefer. With wisdom born of experience, we are motivated to let go of the bad habits and keep the good ones. This is a deeper and more enduring training than getting rid of the bad habits while they are first forming.

The prodigal, upon his conscious return from the far country, becomes an even more devoted son of his father. The disparity between the dead-end road he was on, and the comfort and nurturing of his father's opulent estate is one he will never forget. This experience will serve him well should he be tempted to stray again.

Identify with the Father

Truth be told, we are all prodigals. We have all left our Father's estate in search of something better. Just like the son in the parable, we will all sooner or later return to our true home. Seeking fulfillment in an impermanent world must eventually frustrate us. The gifts the world promises are alluring but ultimately unsatisfying. The question is not whether we will make the crucial U-turn, but when, and how much suffering we are willing to put up with before the light bulb flashes over our head and we realize how good we had it before we decided to seek reality in a world of illusions. *A Course in Miracles* tells us, "Tolerance for pain may be high, but it is not without limit." While it may take us a certain amount of frustration and despair before we change direction, the road to home is always open. Our Father is not daunted by our impudence. Instead, He welcomes us with open arms.

While we may identify with the righteous son and/or the prodigal, the paramount teaching of the parable is for us to identify with the compassionate, forgiving father. We are called to allow his voice to take center stage in our mind. Our soul remains established in our heavenly home even while elements of our personality squander their energy in riotous living or resentfully follow endless rules. To return to the father's estate is to become the father and leave behind all lesser identities. Our higher self embraces all parts of our earthly expression, recognizes the good we do, and accepts us when we have messed up. Jesus Christ maintained that expansive identity, and through this timeless parable, he calls us to do the same.

THE TRUE MEANING
OF FORGIVENESS

When Pam's husband Tom had an affair, his girlfriend became pregnant. "Tom came to me, explained the situation, and told me that he deeply regretted the affair and he wanted to renew our marriage," Pam told me. "I sensed that Tom was sincere, so I accepted him. When we both realized that the baby's mother was mentally ill and would be an unfit mother, we decided to take the child and raise her as our own."

Many wives would not have been so compassionate to their husband and his "illegitimate" baby. (Yet every child is legitimate in the eyes of God.) Such a wife might say, "You cheated on me. This is your problem, not mine." Yet Pam dropped into a deeper place in her heart and wanted the baby to have a healthy upbringing. She achieved an extraordinary act of forgiveness.

We all deal with unforgiving thoughts and feelings. The disciple Peter came to Jesus and asked, "When someone wrongs me, how many times should I forgive him? Seven times?" Jesus answered, "Not seven. Seventy times seven."

Jesus followed his answer with one of his most poignant parables:

A king was settling his accounts with his servants when he discovered that a servant to whom he had loaned a huge sum of money had not repaid him. The king summoned the servant and told him that because he had failed to resolve his debt, he would be sold into slavery. The servant became terrified, dropped to his knees, and begged the king to have mercy. The king was touched and filled with compassion, so he forgave the servant the entire debt.

Later the king learned that the servant he had forgiven had loaned a fellow servant a tiny sum of money, and when he did not repay, the lender had him thrown into prison. Hearing this, the king became angry with the servant he had forgiven, and had him severely punished until he repaid his debt to the king.

In *A Course in Miracles*, Jesus neatly sums up this parable:

> God offers only mercy. Your words should reflect
> only mercy, because that is what you have
> received and that is what you should give.

We are all the servant who owes the king a huge debt—or at least we believe we do. Through unconscious living and accumulated errors, we have all run up a massive karmic debt that, according to reincarnation teachers, will take us many lifetimes to pay off. But Jesus Christ overturned the law of karma and replaced it with the Law of Grace. If we were all required to do strict penance for our sins, we would be in deep trouble and stay stuck on the karmic wheel for eons. But Jesus Christ introduced us to a God of mercy, not retribution. His entire ministry was devoted to freeing humanity from the burden of belief in sin and punishment, and restoring to us our original innocence. He said, "My grace is sufficient for you."

The volume of forgiveness Jesus prescribed to Peter, "seventy times seven," does not represent an actual number. Jesus did not mean, "After you have forgiven four hundred and ninety times, go right ahead and mete out punishment." The term "seventy times seven" means "unlimited." There's is no end to the amount of forgiveness we are to extend. The message is: *Just keep forgiving.*

A Higher View of Forgiveness

A Course in Miracles tells us that the notion of forgiveness most people hold is quite limited and does not penetrate to the depth of the gifts that genuine forgiveness delivers. We usually take forgiveness to mean, "You did something really bad that damaged me. But I will be magnanimous and overlook the pain you caused."

This view keeps both the forgiver and the perpetrator in a psychic jail. It implies that the victim is small, powerless, and vulnerable to the indiscreet acts of a cruel individual. It also implies that one person has the power to determine another person's experience. This may be so in the story of the world, but the story of the world just keeps spinning in painful cycles from which humanity has failed to escape. Villain, victim, retaliation, separation, pain, sorrow . . . Villain, victim, retaliation, separation, pain, sorrow . . . and on and on and on. This is the drama upon which humanity's history is built, except for rare instances when someone rises above the old story and chooses a new one.

The new story is a higher view of forgiveness:

I am an eternal, powerful, invulnerable expression of God. I create my experience by the thoughts and attitudes I hold. You do not have the power to take away my happiness unless I give it to you. I now take back the power I gave you to hurt me. My true self is untouchable and safe. What you did seemed to hurt me only because I interpreted your actions as victimizing me. I no longer choose to see myself as a victim of your actions, or the actions of anyone. I am an independent, sovereign creator of my life. I now release you from the act I held against you. I set myself free, along with you, and I move on to a joyful and empowered life.

This version of forgiveness is far more affirming than to believe that others can give you happiness or take it away. Here lies the liberation we have been longing for.

Freeing Others Frees Yourself

In the parable of the ungrateful servant, mercy means to release another person from their debt to you. This dynamic runs far beyond money. When we refuse to forgive, in our mind we hold the other person in a state of indebtedness. Their karmic bank account is in the red. We hold a sword to their throat and threaten to return the pain they have caused us, and sometimes we do. Or we hope they are punished by "poetic justice." Yet there is no poetry in punishment. The only real poetry is forgiveness.

The attitude of debt and punishment ultimately backfires because the moment we throw the book of karma at the other person, we throw it at ourself. If they are subject to caustic retribution for their sin, so are we. Here is where Jesus shines as the master psychologist. You will not escape the judgments you lay on others. When you drop into the consciousness of judgment, everyone and everything is judgeable, including yourself. Only in the delusion of ego can you project your sins onto other people and escape them yourself. In the act of judgment, you dive into the torturous world of sin and punishment, which makes hell on Earth for those who give it as well as those who receive it. When you throw someone into the jail of condemnation, you have to sit at the door of their cell to make sure they do not escape. So you are in prison along with the person you have incarcerated.

In some Bible translations, the ungrateful servant is "delivered to the tormentors." This is an apt description of what happens when you hold a grudge. You remain subject to your own tormenting thoughts, and you are the one who suffers. The person you fail to forgive is not hurt in the least by your lack of forgiveness. They may be out having a good time while you suffer. "Resentment is like taking a spoonful of poison and then waiting for the other person to die." Resentment hurts the resentor far more than the object of resentment.

God is not a punishing God. We are punishing humans. Some metaphysical teachers replace the term "the Lord" with "the Law." This removes the very primitive image of God as an old bald man with a long white beard sitting on a distant cloud throwing gumdrops to a few lucky people and casting lightning bolts at others. If you don't like the idea of God as a person, reframe God as a principle. The Law of Mind says that when you wish ill for another, you wish ill for yourself. When you wish well for others, you wish well for yourself. When Jesus said, "Judge not, that you be not judged," he was talking about a psychological dynamic more than a cosmic court system. When we show mercy, we receive mercy, because what we give to others, we give to ourself in the moment we give it.

Forgiveness as Release

The word "forgiveness" is highly charged for many people because they believe that to forgive will cause them to somehow lose. I like to substitute the word, "release," which has a very positive and freeing connotation. When you release something, you get lighter and happier—exactly what happens when you forgive.

If you have a hard time forgiving, practice this visualization:

> Imagine before you a radiant golden or white light (or any soothing color). Then in your mind take a small object like a pen or a cup, and hold it up to the light. Say to yourself, "I release this _____ to the light." Then imagine that the object merges into the light and disappears.

> After practicing with a few simple objects, release some elements of your life that you find difficult. "I release this project to the light." "I release the pain in my arm to the light." "I release my financial situation to the light." As you visualize these situations disappearing into a bright, beautiful, healing field of energy, you will feel happier, lighter, and freer, and the situation you designate will cease to oppress you.

> When you have gotten into the flow of the exercise, take someone you have a hard time with, and release that person to the light. Observe their face, physical features, and personality characteristics, and say, "I release [Name of Person] and our relationship to the light." Keep breathing deeply, relaxing, and visualize your history with them or any way you think about them as merging into the light, until that person and your relationship disappears, and only light remains. This vision of that person reflects their true nature as a kindred soul.

If you do this exercise sincerely, you will feel relieved of the burden your relationship represents to you, and you will likely experience some manifestation of your elevated consciousness.

What you just did was an act of forgiveness. You did not make that person's sin solid and then try to get rid of it. Instead, you let their sin dissolve into the great All That Is. You can resolve all of your forgiveness issues without using the word "forgive" if you prefer. Forgiveness is release, by whatever name you call it. "Forgiveness" is "for giving," not for keeping.

Your Investment in Your Own Salvation

You have been told that when you show mercy, mercy will be shown to you. This is true not because when you are a good person, God will reward you; that is a very elementary interpretation of the Law of Mind. When you show mercy, mercy will be shown to you because you have established your mind in a merciful state of consciousness. The Law of Attraction draws to us people and experiences that mirror the thoughts we hold. To give mercy catapults you into a world of mercy. When you mete out punishment, you ensnare yourself in a mindset of guilt. Mercy removes you from that nasty domain and plants your feet on the lawns of heaven.

You will expect others to do to you what you do to them, for better or worse. Kind people expect to be treated kindly and, for the most part, they are. Nasty people expect to be treated rudely, and, for the most part, they are. Every act you generate makes you equivalent to every act that matches it.

Giving mercy, then, or forgiving, is the strongest investment you can make in your own salvation, salvation being release from suffering. You don't need to pray to God to release you from your suffering, although that's a good start. God has already released you. Now you must release yourself by not doing anything that causes anyone—including yourself—to suffer. They are your own self in a disguised form. What you do to them, you do to yourself.

What the recipient of your forgiveness does with your gift is not your business. That person may accept your offering, or they may refuse it. That doesn't matter. If they cannot accept your forgiveness, or they continue to hold a grudge against you, they have their own inner work to do. Meanwhile, you have done what you have to do. You are right with yourself and with God. The Creator can ask no more of you.

God has already forgiven your debt. The Force of Love has torn up your mortgage and inscribed your name on the deed to your divine estate. You don't owe God anything except gratitude. In the spiritual accounting system, you have always been solvent, and you always will be. It is only in the world of illusion that we play the game of debt. The way to let yourself off the hook is to let others off the hook. Then you become the grateful—and free—servant of a well-pleased king. Eventually, as you became the welcoming father in the parable of the prodigal son, you become the forgiving king in the parable that is your life.

LOG OUT

A mentally troubled man regularly rides a bicycle through our neighborhood and yells at people driving by. He believes that auto exhaust is polluting the environment, and no one should use a car. He even sprayed a can of Mace at a woman through her open car window. He has been in and out of jail.

One day while I was taking a walk, this fellow approached me. I tried to ignore him, but he began to talk to me. "Do you think I can save this salamander?" he asked me as he showed me a little creature in his hand. "It looks like it is dehydrated," he remarked as he gently stroked its back. "I am taking it to the lake. I hope it will drink and feel better." He shrugged and added, "Even if it doesn't survive, it is God's creature. Like all of us, it has eternal life." With that, he smiled, told me, "Have a good day," and went on his way, cradling the salamander in one hand as he steered his bike with the other.

I stopped in my tracks. While I had strong judgments against this man and I recoiled in his presence, there was an aspect of him that was gentle and loving, even Christlike. He wasn't simply a whacko. He had a good heart. I was touched and inspired by this person I had written off as unlovable.

> Why do you look at the speck of sawdust in your brother's eye and pay no attention to the log in your own eye? How can you say to your brother, "Let me take the speck out of your eye," when all the time there is a log in your own eye? You hypocrite, first take the log out of your own eye, and then you will see clearly how to remove the speck from your brother's eye.

It is tempting to try to correct other people rather than correcting ourselves. The campaign to change others is a distraction from facing our own issues. When we do not want to see an unwanted trait or behavior in ourself, we project it onto others. Then we believe we have to fix or manipulate their behavior, or get rid of them, rather than address our own fears and limiting beliefs. This is the ego's ruse to disown our shadow. We turn certain individuals, genders, ethnic groups, religions, races, or nationalities into the devil and then wage a war to fix them or purge them from our experience. But the war is not out there. It is in here. We will never win the outer battle because we are fighting our shadow self. Sally Kempton said, "It's hard to fight an enemy who has outposts in your head."

The Great Ink Blot Test

The world is a huge ink blot test, revealing what we are project-ing onto it. I attended a spiritual conference where a lecturer presented slides illustrating her lesson. One of the slides included a drawing of a slot machine. Seeing that image, a woman in the audience stood and shouted, "That proves it! You are an agent of the anti-Christ! Your last slide displayed '666'— the mark of the beast!"

Taken aback, the lecturer backed up to the slide, which showed the slot machine with three cherries in its windows. It took a huge stretch of the imagination to interpret the cher-ries as "666"—but the woman who objected did exactly that. It was obvious to everyone in the audience that the intention was to present cherries, not numbers, and they laughed at the suggestion.

When you are looking for the anti-Christ, you can find it if you try hard enough. If you are looking for the Christ, you can also find that. *A Course in Miracles* tells us that everyone we meet is the Christ seeking to be revealed. That revelation comes from the vision we are using. We see what we choose to see and we ignore all else. As Dale Carnegie stated, "Two men looked out from prison bars. One saw mud, the other saw stars."

Enjoy the View

In the last chapter, we focused in the futility of judging others. Yet the most important judgment to release is self-judgment. Any judgment you hold of others is a projection of judgment of self. If you sincerely forgave yourself, you would simultane-ously drop your judgments of the world and be free of them all.

Many of us are brutally hard on ourselves. We beat ourselves up for the smallest perceived offense. If we do a task ninety--nine percent well and one percent not so well, we remember the one percent and berate ourself for failing. Most people hold a higher opinion of us than we hold of ourself. If we could just appreciate ourself as much as others value us, we would move forward at lightning speed!

The Dove soap company sponsored a fascinating experiment. The organizers asked a number of women to describe themselves to a forensic artist, who could not see them as they sat behind a curtain. The artist drew a portrait of each woman based on her self-description. Then another woman who had just met the subject model described the woman to the artist, and he drew the observer's description. When the artist held the two pictures of the subject model side by side, the difference was staggering! The women's self-described portraits were uncomplimentary and rather ugly. The portraits as described by the observer were lovely and attractive. (YouTube: *Dove Real Beauty Sketches*) Others see far more beauty and good in us than we see in ourselves. It is said, "A friend is someone who sees through you and enjoys the view."

Jesus taught, "Love your neighbor as yourself." We usually interpret the golden rule as an admonition to be kinder to others. Yet few people seek to balance the equation by being as kind to themselves as they are to others. We extend gratitude, service, and forgiveness to others that we withhold from ourselves. We overlook their mistakes and urge our loved ones to take better care of themselves and hasten toward their dreams. Meanwhile we push ourselves to exhaustion or illness, and we postpone doing the things that would make us happy. If we gave ourselves the same acceptance and encouragement we give our loved ones, we would truly be applying the golden rule!

The reason you should not judge is that you *cannot* judge. You have no idea how a particular act fits into the greater plan of your life or another's. Some huge mistake for which you condemn yourself may turn out to be a powerful asset. It takes trust and patience to allow ourselves to discover the truth, even if we make errors along the way. The record books never show the score at halftime.

Discernment, Not Judgment

Releasing judgment does not mean that we take license to do unkind things, or we should put up with abuse. We need to release judgment, but retain discernment. Discernment is the ability to distinguish between wise and foolish actions. If you are asked to do something that grates against your conscience, you must decline. If you see an act of abuse occurring to another, you must not condone it. If you have a significant life choice to make, and one alternative speaks to your heart more strongly than another, you must choose in accord with your inner compass. Saying "no" to what is not right for you clears the way for what truly matches you.

How do you know the difference between judgment and discernment? Judgment carries an emotional charge. If you are upset about someone's behavior or some situation, you have dropped into judgment. Judgment is fueled by fear, as is all upset. Do your best to never act when you are upset. Your action will likely backfire, and you will have to retrace your steps and choose again, this time from your higher mind rather than base emotions.

Discernment is founded on calm inner guidance. You may take the same actions as you might take when you judge, but there is no emotional charge and no fear-based resistance or karmic backlash. You perceive the path that matches your guidance and intention, and you follow it. You trust that if you are following your true inner voice, everyone will be served. When you act from discernment, your choices work and you advance firmly on your path.

A Sophisticated Psychology Lesson

The metaphor of removing the log from your own eye rather than attempting to remove the speck from your brother's eye is a sophisticated lesson in psychology. In just a few words, Jesus gave the key for humanity to eliminate conflict and bloodshed. If we owned the traits we fight to expunge from others, and examined our own fears rather than leveraging blame, there would be no murder, war, or genocide. If people who hate others healed their own self-hatred, they would be relieved of the torment of detesting others or needing to control or get rid of them.

If you find yourself growing angry at someone or judging them, ask yourself what fear their behavior has touched in you. Anger is fear under pressure. When you identify the underlying fear and hold it up to the light of higher awareness, your upset will dissipate and you will know exactly how to deal with that person. He or she may remain in your world, but you will no longer lose your peace in their presence. Or that person may spin out of your experience. Either way, you will be free of the upset you felt with them. Healing relationships is an inside job.

If you find yourself judging another person, ask yourself if you ever do the act you are judging them for. In most cases, the answer will be yes. Or you so vehemently fear or hate this behavior that you identify with its opposite. This process of self-inquiry requires honesty and a strong intention to get free. If you can accept your role in your upset, and love and accept yourself even with your unwanted trait, you are well on your way to healing all of your relationships.

Jesus Christ did not advise us to run away from life, but rather to take the nitty-gritty situations of life—especially relationships—and apply higher wisdom to them so we escape the pain that many relationships yield. He does not ask us to be saints, but simply to be willing to do our part to heal difficult interactions. We cannot afford to wait until the other person makes an overture toward healing. We must initiate change by fearlessly looking within. When we have healed our own fear-based judgments, only then can we say we are free.

A HIGHER LAW

In graduate school I served as assistant to the Dean of Students. My first assignment was to respond to companies requesting recommendations for graduates who had applied for jobs. In most cases this was an easy task, as the students had done well in their studies and I could recommend them with confidence.

Then I received a request regarding a student who had done quite poorly in college. He had gotten bad grades, flunked out, and then returned. His record showed that he was antisocial, he had gotten into fights, and had been placed on probation. He barely made it through college to graduate. In my opinion, he did not at all deserve a recommendation.

When I showed my proposed rejection response to Dean Blanton, he paged through the student's file and smiled softly.

"Let's just write him a recommendation," he said. "We'll give the guy a chance."

As I re-drafted my response, I realized I had been given a teaching that far surpassed the psychology classes I was studying in. Dean Blanton bypassed the student's errors and replaced condemnation with forgiveness. He wanted to help the student more than penalize him. To this day, many years later, that interaction stands as one of my most important memories of my education.

Grace Supersedes Karma

The mystical messiah delivered one of his most penetrating teachings when he was confronted with a woman caught in the act of adultery. A mob of angry men chased the woman to a wall in Jerusalem near where Jesus sat. As the men picked up stones to murder the adulteress, one man told the master, "The law teaches that the penalty for this woman's sin is death. What do you say?"

Jesus sat quietly, carving a circle in the dirt with his finger. Finally he responded, "Let the first stone be cast by the one among you who is without sin." Hearing this, one by one the men dropped their rocks and walked away.

"Who has condemned you now?" Jesus asked the woman, tears streaming down her cheeks.

The woman looked up at the empty square. "No one, sir."

"Neither do I condemn you," he told her. "Go and sin no more."

From a human standpoint, we are all sinners. We have all violated the laws of religion, society, and morality. If we were to be held to the letter of the law, we all deserve punishment.

Yet Jesus Christ demonstrated a higher law. Grace overlooks our errors and, as Dean Blanton advised, "Let's give this guy a chance." The spiritual master Paramahansa Yogananda, author of the classic *Autobiography of a Yogi*, said, "The Law of Grace supersedes the law of karma." Compassion is more powerful than retribution. If punishment were the final justice, we would all be in big trouble. Mahatma Gandhi said, "'An eye for an eye and a tooth for a tooth' will leave the whole world blind and toothless." Jesus taught, "the heart of the law is mercy." He called us to live by that principle rather than the harsh rules we have fabricated.

Freedom for the Accuser

In this incident, Jesus brought healing not just to the woman, but to the irate crowd. Embroiled in their anger and rage to punish, they did not realize that the murder would taint their souls even more than the woman's act of adultery would hurt her or her husband. Christ's release of the woman saved the angry mob from the burdensome karma they would generate for themselves. Any accuser, while apparently righteous, suffers as much as the person he or she punishes, perhaps more. The sinner's error is singular and obvious; the accuser's anger ravages that person subconsciously and continually. The ego tells us that casting judgment on another will free us from our own guilt— but it only drives guilt deeper. Had those men killed that woman, they would have walked away steeped in "righteous" judgment—the tip of the iceberg of self-judgment—which would torture them until they grew beyond a condemnation mentality. In releasing the adulteress and turning the mob away, Christ saved them both.

Which Character Do You Own?

While this anecdote seems to be one vignette in a biblical saga, it is more fundamentally an x-ray of the dynamics of our mind. The sinner, the accuser, and the liberator each play their part in our psyche. The sinner has violated social or religious law; the accuser points the finger of guilt; and the liberator erases the violation and saves the sinner from punishment, while freeing the accuser from inner turmoil.

Which character do you identify with? You might think of yourself as the sinner waiting to be punished. Or you might identify with the angry mob, ready to mete out retribution. We go through our days alternating between feeling guilty and punishing the guilty—both sides of the same coin. Neither of these approaches works because feeling guilty and leveraging guilt both leave us stuck in hell.

The character we are ultimately called to identify with is the liberator, expressed by Jesus. He wants us to see the situation from his higher vantage point, and free ourselves as well as those we judge. While in the worldly drama we tend to embody our social roles, on the broader stage we are called to accept our divine role. *That* is the greatest story ever told.

The Higher GPS

Finally Jesus told the woman, "Go and sin no more." His forgiveness of her adultery was not a blanket license for her or us to continue engaging in behaviors that hurt ourselves or others. He was saying, "I want you to have a better life. Please take good care of yourself and don't put yourself or others in painful situations. I love you enough to redirect you."

A Course in Miracles distinguishes between a sin and an error. We have all made plenty of errors, but we have never sinned. A sin implies that we have offended God and we deserve to be hurt in return. But we cannot offend God because God is love and only love, and love does not take offense. Only ego takes offense. We do not deserve punishment any more than the adulteress did. I recount the word "sin" only because that is the term English language bibles use. The word derives from the original Aramaic, Hebrew, and Greek languages. It is an archery term meaning, "to miss the target." So a sin simply means we have strayed from our path. It is a not a signal of condemnation, but a call to get back on course.

If you are using a GPS navigator to guide you to a destination, and you veer from the suggested route, the GPS voice simply says, "rerouting," and then provides directions from the point where you now stand. The GPS does not get emotionally involved and say, "You idiot! Why didn't you follow my directions? You are in big trouble now! You didn't listen to me, so I am not going to help you anymore. The Lord will punish you for violating my instructions!"

How silly it would be for the GPS to take personally you not heeding its directions. That's because the GPS operates by non-emotional scientific principles. The system is more interested in helping you get where you want to go than having an ego meltdown so it can prove it is right, or chastise you for your error. Any of those behaviors would be a waste of time and energy—exactly what guilt is. Instead, the GPS simply implies, "Let's start over from where we are now." We might substitute the GPS initials for, "God's Program for Salvation," salvation meaning rerouting from what causes us pain, and course correcting toward what brings us peace.

A Call for Love

A Course in Miracles tells us that every human action is either a pure expression of love or a call of love. We can reframe anti-social, unkind, and dysfunctional behaviors as a call of love. Jesus regarded the woman's act of adultery as an unskillful way to get the love she felt she was missing in her marriage. There are healthier ways to get love. The love that she sought from an external source was already inside her.

We are all searching for love. Sometimes we look for it in the right places and find it, and at other times we look for it elsewhere and miss it. In forgiving the adulteress, Jesus was demonstrating that she came to the right place for love. We can each be the right place that others come to for love. The same God that loved that woman through Jesus will love the "sinners" in your life through you. That same love will comfort you when you believe you are a sinner. The master was modeling how we should treat people whom others would condemn—including ourselves.

One day while Dee and I were walking our dogs, one of the dogs lingered behind us. From time to time I stopped and called him to keep up with the group. Then Dee noticed that he was biting at one of his paws. We stopped and examined his paw, which we discovered had a sticker in it. That's why he was walking slowly and hesitating. We removed the sticker, and he happily caught up with the group.

Anyone who exhibits antisocial behavior has a sticker in his or her paw. Meanspirited dogs have been abused. So it is with people. Healthy people do not hurt others; that is an unnatural act. Only people in pain pass their angst along to others. "Hurt people hurt people." When confronted with an obnoxious person, if we can just stop for a moment, take a breath, avoid a knee-jerk reaction, and remember, "this person is in pain," we can serve as a healer rather than perpetuating the chain of karma.

Feed My Sheep

When Jesus appeared to the disciple Peter after the resurrection, he asked Peter, "Do you love me?" Peter answered, "Yes." Jesus asked the question two more times, and Peter again answered in the affirmative. Jesus replied, "Then feed my sheep." Some people take this injunction literally, and provide meals for hungry people—a truly blessed service. Yet more fundamentally, Jesus wants us to feed the souls of his sheep, the family of humanity. Every time you affirm the value of someone you encounter, you are feeding his or her soul. Most people feel in some way unworthy or sinful, so when you see the God in them rather than evil, you neutralize the illusion that keeps them in pain. When you treat them as an angel rather than a convict, you are invoking a higher law, which can create the transformation of a lifetime. We all just want to know that we are loveable. All else is detail.

PERFECT NOW

As the cashier scanned my groceries at the food market, I noticed that she was an extraordinarily attractive woman. Jennifer's long, thick hair, creamy skin, fit figure, angelic face, and clear, sparking eyes were stunning. Beyond her physical appearance, she radiated vibrant health. She could easily have been a cover model for a major women's magazine.

A few weeks later I was quite surprised to see Jennifer in the audience of a seminar where I was a guest speaker. My friend Nora was presenting a series of classes for women who wanted to feel better about their body self-image. At one point Nora asked each participant to share what she liked most and least about her body. Jennifer took the microphone. "I hate my belly," she said. "When I look in the mirror I feel so fat and ugly."

I was floored. I don't think Jennifer had one extra ounce of fat on her body, including her belly. This woman who was

117

perfectly beautiful according to societal images had severe judgments about her body. Something was really wrong with this picture.

From Frustration to Celebration

When we hear Jesus's teaching, "Be perfect, even as your Father in heaven is perfect," we may feel more irritated than inspired. It seems as if Christ is setting us up to lose, since no human being is perfect or ever will be. Even if you are perfect in some way, Jennifer demonstrated that the judgmental mind creeps to the forefront and sabotages our vision of our deep inherent beauty.

Trying to become perfect is exasperating and exhausting, the frustrating dilemma of the Greek mythological figure Sisyphus, who kept rolling a rock to the top of a hill, only to have it keep rolling back to him. You can execute perfectly for a moment, but quickly you find yourself back in the anxious gap between where you are and where you think you should be. In the human condition, perfection is the impossible dream.

Yet if we look more deeply into Jesus's instruction, he was setting us up to win. As in the beatitudes, the key word is, "Be." He didn't say "Become perfect." Becoming perfect throws our consciousness into an imaginary, never-present future. "Being," on the other hand, is a now condition. Jesus was teaching the ultimate metaphysical lesson: *You are already perfect. Now just know it and live it.*

The perfection Jesus was pointing to is not of our humanity. It is of our divinity. While your body, personality, or relationship track record may be far from perfect, your spiritual nature is absolutely pristine—always has been, always is, and always will be. We have been looking for perfection where it does not

exist. The place to look is into our soul, where God dwells in
utter majesty as us.

Here ends the impossible task of improving yourself.
You cannot fix what is not broken, or improve on God's
idea. Self-improvement is a myth. Your true Self does not
need improvement. It needs *recognition*. Our goal is self-
realization. Enlightenment is not a change in conditions, but
a change in mind. Seen through the eyes of imperfection,
everything we look upon is faulty, including ourselves. Seen
through the eyes of perfection, everything we see is a miracle,
including ourselves.

Ripe for Harvest Now

Jesus Christ used the language of his time to impart wisdom to
his audience. If he taught today, he might speak of parallel realities, nonphysical dimensions, or quantum physics. Instead, he
used metaphors his contemporaries could understand. When
we return to our innocent mind, we can understand them, too.
In three short sentences Christ captured the secret of all healing and achievement:

> You say, "still four months until the fields
> are white with harvest." I say, "look up!
> The fields are ripe for harvest now."

The key to this profound directive lies in the instruction,
"look up." Jesus was not referring to physical eyesight, but inner
vision. He was urging us to see from a higher perspective. We
proceed *from* blessing, not *toward* it. We must not strive for
completion; we must own it. We cannot afford to postpone the

life we would live. We must live it where we stand. Tomorrow is an illusion; it never comes. Only the now exists.

Jesus was undoing the fundamental trick of the ego, which is to create a distance between ourselves and fulfillment. The trickster tells us that what we seek lives at a distance in time or space; we must travel to an exotic site or wait until a momentous date before we can be happy. But as we sit and wait for the planets to align, we miss the alignment that already exists. The gem of truth is not hidden in a secret cave or ruled by stars; it is firmly established in our heart. The harvest we have attributed to elsewhere or the future is here now. "In this day the scripture is fulfilled."

As you catch Christ's expansive vision, a sleeping giant begins to stir within you. If you knew you were already blessed, and the things you most deeply desire are available to you, what would you be doing differently? Would you give up anxious striving? Would you drop your sense of unworthiness, and love who and what you see in the mirror? Would you act on your exciting visions rather than waiting for others to approve? Would you dwell in constant, ecstatic gratitude?

Many people have a "bucket list," the things they hope to do before they die. While these goals are fun and worth pursuing, the real bucket is not the one we need to fill. It is the container of good we already carry. What could you add to your bucket if you knew it was already full? The real bucket is not filled with doing, but being. Whether or not you do all the things you hope to do is less important than your state of mind while you do them, or don't. Your "to do" list is not nearly as important as your "to be" list.

When Hamlet contemplated, "To be, or not to be, that is the question," he was not just referring to whether he would continue his life or end it. Shakespeare seeded a stunning meta-physical teaching in that one verse. Are you going to enjoy your being, or deny it? Are you going to live now, or wait for something better to happen? Will your happiness depend on external events, or will you source your joy from a place deep inside you? We all face Hamlet's dilemma daily. Playwright George Bernard Shaw answered Hamlet's question:

> Life is no brief candle to me. It is a sort of splendid torch which I have got a hold of for the moment, and I want to make it burn as brightly as possible before handing it on to future generations.

Done is Better than Perfect

Many people use perfectionism as a defense mechanism to avoid the judgment they fear if they exposed themselves or their work to public view. "If I just keep polishing the book I am writing, I won't have to show it to the world, and face criticism or rejection." So we keep our good work hidden and use prolonged fixing as an excuse to avoid humiliation. In delaying presenting yourself or your work to the world, you avoid failure, but you also avoid success. While not everyone will like or approve of what you do, some people, perhaps many, will applaud your offering. You will add value to the lives of your audience. Don't withhold the gifts which God has entrusted you to deliver to the world because you have allowed ego to hijack your self-image. When you partner with God and release your work to the world as an offering to bless others, miracles will happen. Spirit will connect you and your work with all the people who can most benefit from it, with the least effort and no struggle on your part.

If you have a project you have been laboring over, consider how free you would feel to get it off your plate and into the hands of the people you can best serve. If you wait until you or your good works are perfect before you deliver them, you may be waiting for a very long time, and miss all the blessings you and others can enjoy now. Your product may not be your ultimate creation, but it is your perfect creation from where you stand. Launching it will lead to more and better.

Even while life is a work in process, there is perfection at each turn. The process is as meaningful as the product. Celebrate the gifts you have been given, and those you are giving, and you will attain mastery on a daily basis.

Perfect Humility

When Jesus advised us to be as perfect as our heavenly Father, he was teaching us to identify with God rather than our human faults and sins. It is not arrogant to claim perfection. It is more arrogant to deny perfection. When you refute wholeness, you are arguing with creation. You are saying that you are less than God created you to be. You are not a perfect human being, but you are a perfect expression of the divine. Quit arguing for your limits and reinforcing the problems of the world. Instead, make a stand for your unlimited nature and the blessings you own. The world is changed by people who see beyond it. Jesus initiated that vision, and now it is up to us to put it into action.

Your experience of life depends on who you think you are. If you are mortal, you cannot be immortal. If you are flawed, you cannot be perfect. If you live inside a bag of skin, you cannot inhabit the cosmos. Every great spiritual master has reminded us of our true identity by peeling away the false identities that have been laid over us. We might call Christ "The Great Revealer."

You are not going to walk in the kingdom of heaven. You are walking in the kingdom of heaven now. If you don't see it, it is only because you are using a different vision than the one that tells of paradise. Jesus Christ's vision was perfect, so he saw only perfection. When we upgrade our vision, we will see as he saw, behold what he beheld, and generate miracles like unto him.

MORE SHALL
BE GIVEN

My client Ben was worried about money. He had quit his corporate job and initiated his hypnotherapy practice, and now he was struggling to pay his bills. He was behind on his mortgage payments and he needed to support his wife and two children. Ben was so stressed that he lost touch with his passion for his new career. "But I can't go back to my old job that grated against my soul," he told me.

In coaching, I helped Ben reclaim his vision and passion. He remembered why he changed careers, and how great he would feel if he succeeded. Ben got so excited that I could see rockets of energy shooting from his face. Back on track with his prosperity mindset, he went on to attract new clients, and he built a successful hypnotherapy practice. The key shift for Ben was moving from his fearful mind to his empowered mind; from what was lacking to what was possible. Everything that happens to us is related to how we think about ourself, what we deserve, and what the universe is capable of supplying.

Many of us worry a little or a lot about prosperity. Can I earn enough to stay afloat? Do I have to sell myself out and take a job I hate in order to earn a substantial income? Must I work with people who do not share my values, or can I create a livelihood with people aligned with my vision? If I have to stay in a job that is less than my ideal, at least for now, can I find a way to enjoy my work and sleep well at night, knowing my hours on the job were well spent? Do I really have to work so much, or can I carve out more time to do the things I love?

Jesus Christ was a master prosperity teacher. Lack and poverty had no place in his mind. His bold statements illuminate the inner dynamics that make our lives abundant. He wants you to mobilize your own divine mind to plumb the riches you deserve. He declared, "It is the Father's good pleasure to give you the kingdom." Everything you need to know about how to be wealthy is revealed in the New Testament.

Given, or Taken Away?

One of Jesus's prosperity principles makes no sense to the reasoning mind:

> Whoever has, will be given more,
> and he will have abundance.
>
> Whoever does not have, even what he has
> will be taken away from him.

MORE SHALL BE GIVEN

How unfair this sounds! Why should the rich get richer, and the poor get poorer? Surely a merciful God would take from the rich and give to the poor. Everyone should enjoy equal wealth, right?

Yet life operates on laws that go far beyond what seems fair to the intellect. Universal principles are fair to everyone because everyone has equal access to them, and everyone can use them in their favor when they understand them. Here is the inner meaning of Jesus's odd statement:

Whatever you focus on, you get more of. Attention is intention. Fascination is fertilizer. Anything you put your mind on expands in your experience. Every thought is a seed that grows more like itself. For this reason, we must focus only on what we wish to have more of.

When you place your attention on supply and abundance, you generate more supply and abundance. When you give attention to lack and loss, you magnify lack and loss in your experience. This is the Law of Mind. You can't bend it, avoid it, substitute for it, or make its opposite true. It's just the way the universe works. We can depend on this principle to work every time in every situation, and employ it in our favor.

My friend Hannah is a very successful entrepreneur. She has several businesses that yield her a huge income. Everything she touches turns to gold. Hannah is marshalling the law to her advantage. I have another friend, Connie, who can hardly make ends meet. Her world pictures one drama after another. Whatever money she gets, goes away. She is constantly struggling to survive.

Hannah is not lucky, and Connie is not cursed. We make our own luck or our own curse by how we use our mind. Connie has access to the same principles that Hannah uses in her favor.

At the moment, Connie is working the law against herself. Both women are demonstrating mastery. Hanna is demonstrating mastery of prosperity and Connie is demonstrating mastery of lack. Same principle, opposite results. In an odd way, poor people are abundant. They are abundant in poverty. Wherever they turn, they see not enough, and they get more and more of not enough. So they are rich in lack!

Even while Connie has a hard time financially, she is a kind and loving person. You would think that God would reward her for her benevolent nature. And God has rewarded her, because her good heart brings her inner peace. But not money. The Bible tells us that "God is no respecter of persons," meaning that God does not favor some people and disfavor others. We favor or disfavor ourselves. The life we create depends on how we apply the scientific law. Though Connie is a dear soul, she is not making use of the law to her financial advantage. One day she will figure it out and work the law in her favor, as we all will.

Some very wealthy people are nasty, narcissistic, and apparently evil. It seems unfair that such mean people should have lots of money and good stuff. But God is no respecter of persons. These individuals have learned to use the Law of Mind to generate fabulous wealth. One day they will hopefully recognize their personality failings and be healed of cruelty. Meanwhile they are working the law to their financial advantage.

This is why Robin Hood programs of taking from the rich and giving to the poor generally don't work. If you give someone money before he or she understands the principles that govern prosperity, the gift of money will go away like the previous money did. The recipient will expand their wealth only when they change their mind. You cannot legislate prosperity, which is an inside job.

The most effective way to eradicate poverty is to heal poverty consciousness by replacing it with a wealth mindset. When thought patterns change, results change. Some people get so sick and tired of poverty that they reach for better. They study, upgrade their thought pattern, work diligently, and change their life entirely. Some highly motivated individuals work their way out of the ghetto and build an extraordinarily successful life. Their transformation began by latching onto universal principles and putting them into action with skill and intention.

Transformational Moments

The three-dimensional world is the playing field on which we practice manifesting prosperity. When a situation arises that tempts you to feel poor, deprived, or limited, that is your golden opportunity to mobilize your prosperity mind. When you do, you will create a shift in your subconscious more transformational than speaking many affirmations. Such an instant is called a "teachable moment."

If, for example, you are prone to think or say, "there are no jobs that match my passion and skills," or "money is tight," or "there are no available partners out there," immediately correct the lack thought or statement. Say, "There is a perfect, soul-rewarding job for me, which provides me with excellent income and benefits." Or, "I am not subject to the economy that many people subscribe to. I create my own thriving economy by my expanded consciousness." Or, "I don't care how many unavailable partners there are. The Law of Attraction connects me with the right partner who matches me."

Affirming supply in the face of the appearance of lack can change a lifetime habit of deficiency thinking. Because supply is real and lack is illusion, recognizing enoughness dissolves the appearance of not-enoughness. Don't use your childhood programming or history of poverty or failure as an excuse to stay stuck. You are not limited by your parents' role model, your relationship record, or any external condition. All freedom and limitation exist only in your mind. Identify and address them where they live, and you open the door to the riches of the universe.

The final key to manifesting prosperity is to move ahead anyway. Don't let thoughts of fear and limitation hold you back. Post your new website, ask that attractive person for a date, or buy a ticket to visit the enchanting country you've dreamed about. Mobilize your vision and show the universe you mean business. When you ignore thoughts of "I can't," "I can" proves itself to be true.

The Secret of the Loaves and Fishes

When Jesus heard that John the Baptist had been killed, he took a boat with his disciples and retreated to a solitary place. Meanwhile a multitude of people—we are told five thousand—followed him. After three days, Jesus grew concerned that these people had nothing to eat. He told several disciples to gather whatever food they had, which amounted to five loaves of bread and two fish. The master took these items and prayed over them, giving thanks to God. Then he asked the disciples to distribute the food to the masses. Miraculously, the loaves and fish were multiplied so everyone was fed. After the meal, the disciples collected seven baskets of leftover pieces. This is the only miracle that Jesus performed that is recorded in all four gospels.

This amazing story is replete with practical lessons. First of all, we see that Jesus had his human side in that he was moved by the passing of John the Baptist. He needed to process the event and pray about it. When an event such as the death of loved one disturbs us, we must step back and work through our grief. All too often after we lose someone dear to us, we distract ourselves from our deeper feelings. But sooner or later we must come to terms with our sense of loss. If Jesus Christ took such care of himself to head for a quiet place, we must be kind enough to ourselves to do the same.

But alas, the mystical messiah was not able to be alone. With thousands of people at his heels, so much for his private retreat! Yet Jesus, master of compassion, did not send them away. Instead, he took care of them and kept them from going hungry. What a grounded, practical teacher he was! He did not ask the people to fast, suffer, or deny themselves. He was intent to sustain their bodies as well as their souls.

The multiplication of the small supply is the miracle to be learned from here. The first thing Jesus did was to give thanks. He did not ask God for the lack of food to be filled; instead, he blessed the food he had. Christ's appreciation of what he had was so strong that his supply increased dramatically. Here we have the key to how to multiply our own prosperity. Be grateful for what you have, and you open the door for more to come.

Finally, there was so much food that after everyone was fed, there were leftovers. God is not just a God of enough. God is a God of surplus. The universe is not stingy; it is extravagant. When you step into abundance consciousness, you have enough not just for yourself, but for many others, and there will still be surplus. God's coffers are bottomless, and as you recognize yourself to be a child of God, so are yours.

Do not heed teachers and teachings that extol poverty as a spiritual path. There was nothing poor about the mind and life of Jesus Christ, and there need be nothing poor about your life. Look up rather than down, and in rather than out. Celebrate riches wherever you turn. When you get into the flow, you will enjoy overflow. The more you have, the more you will be given. Then you will be a living example of Christ's stunning teaching that prosperity lives right where you stand.

HOW TO GET YOUR
TAXES PAID EASILY

One day the temple tax collectors cornered the disciple Peter and asked him if Jesus had contributed to the temple tax. Peter hastily answered, "Yes," and then returned to the master. Before Peter even spoke, Jesus asked him, "Do the children of a king pay taxes, or does the king collect taxes from other people?" Peter answered, "From other people." To keep the peace and not offend the tax collectors, Jesus instructed Peter to fish in a lake, where the first fish he found would contain a coin in its mouth, worth the precise amount of the tax due.

In this unusual story, Jesus gave Peter—and us—two important messages: First, those who know themselves as children of God live in an exalted dimension far beyond laws made by people. Jesus was calling Peter to a crucial identity shift—from a human being under human laws, to a divine being under only God's laws. The laws of heaven ensure our eternal freedom and unlimited abundance. Laws that people make are largely fear- and lack-based. Our true self can never be taxed.

The second teaching is that Jesus did not want to ruffle the feathers of the tax collectors, so he set up a miraculous scenario where Peter would find the money to pay on Jesus's behalf. This was a brilliant win-win plan. The tax collectors would be satis- fied, and the disciples would not have to struggle to find the tax money.

Here again we see what a practical teacher Jesus was! He kept his head in the clouds and his feet on the ground. He also instructed his disciples, "I am sending you out as sheep among wolves. Be as clever as serpents but as gentle as doves."

Supported by an Abundant Universe

There is an even deeper lesson to this story: The universe is brilliant in its ability to supply all of our needs. If you get a tax or other unexpected or seemingly unfair bill, your divine source will help you pay it. "The Lord is my shepherd. I shall not want." God's treasury is deeper than any human demand. If you resist the bill, worry about it, argue over it, or paint yourself as a victim, your resistance will issue a psychic smoke screen that will prevent or delay your supply from reaching you. If, instead, you relax and trust, the stream of well-being will find you, often in miraculous ways.

There is a rhythm to abundance. Sometimes money pours in, and sometimes it flows out. This cycle is intrinsic to healthy economic and psychological circulation. Be comfortable at both the crest and the trough of the wave. For everything that goes out, something will come in. If you start to worry about money, go to the seashore and observe the ebb and flow of the waves. Notice that when a wave leaves the shore, another one soon touches it. The ocean is far broader than any single wave. Meditate on the vastness and depth of the ocean, and you will recognize the expansiveness of God's storehouse of supply.

Affirm:

God is the source of my supply.

The universe takes care of all of my needs
in wondrous and miraculous ways.

I am open to receive my good through any and
all channels that Higher Power designates.

I am always loved and cared for.

One Source, Many Avenues

Jesus Christ wants his disciples to thrive, not just survive. Jesus did not tell Peter, "Well, you'd better go out and get a second job so you can pay our tax bill." To the contrary, Jesus set up a scenario where Peter could get the necessary resources in the easiest, most graceful way.

Struggle is alien to the teachings of Jesus Christ. He said, "My yoke is easy and my burden is light." It's time to revisit our belief in sacrifice as the road to happiness. Peter lost nothing in getting the tax paid. Many of us were raised with a "no pain, no gain" mentality. A more appropriate maxim would be, "no pain, no pain."

The image of catching the fish containing the coin is also symbolic. You may not find your tax money in the mouth of a fish, but Spirit can provide for you in all kinds of clever ways. The universe might send you a better job, more clients, or a lucrative contract. A new idea of how to expand your business might flash into your brain. You might find someone who can help fund your project, or a smart agent who can get your book, song, or movie produced. You might encounter a traffic jam and take an alternate route to your destination, along which you see a "for sale" sign on the perfect house you have been searching for. You might attend a seminar and take the only empty seat next to someone who becomes your life partner. There are an infinite number of ways the universe can prosper you. Don't get hung up on one particular way, or the details of how you are going to succeed. When you follow your divine intuition, you will be at the right lake at the right time, and the right fish will find you.

The Power of a Wealthy Mind

When Jesus said, "I am come that they might have life, and that they might have it more abundantly," he was not referring simply to money. Money is just one expression of abundance. The deeper meaning of Jesus's statement is, "I want you to feel rich down to your core, and recognize the blessings pouring to you at all times from all directions."

Some books, teachers, and seminars show you how to make more money, which is helpful. Yet the best teachings show you how to transform your mind so you know you are wealthy by nature. You deserve vast riches because of your birthright. You do not work for a king. You are the child of a king. You are rich not because of your bank account, but because of who you are. Even if you do not have a lot of money at a given moment, you may be wealthy in a loving family, good health, inspiring ideas, a passionate career, the beauty of nature, dear friends, loyal pets, creative hobbies, and a spiritual path that gives your life purpose and meaning. You are already affluent in so many ways! Focus on finance where you need to, but keep your vision on the big picture.

You may believe that if you had more money, you would feel rich. And that is so. But if you can get the feeling of being rich now, the Law of Attraction will draw riches unto you, often in the form of money. Metaphysical masters do not wait for the thing to get the feeling. They understand that the feeling magnetizes the thing. They dwell in the experience before the form makes itself obvious.

Whose Picture?

Some government spies tried to catch Jesus advising people to break rules. When they asked Jesus, "Should we pay taxes to the Romans?" Jesus requested they show him a coin. "Whose picture and name are on the coin?" he asked. "Caesar's," they replied. "Then render unto Caesar what is Caesar's, and render unto God what is God's."

We live in a universe where many realities exist simultaneously. In Caesar's kingdom, money and materiality were important, even unto becoming gods. In Spirit's kingdom, inner peace is the coin of the realm. Jesus was advising us to play the money game where necessary, but to keep our eyes on the higher prize. Give materially-minded people what they want, and give God what God wants. God doesn't collect taxes.

God collects only love. When you abide in a state of love, you will be taken care of on Earth as it is in heaven.

Tax-Free Living

We've all heard the maxim, "The only sure things in life are death and taxes." Yet there is far more to life than death and taxes. One of my favorite book titles is *Death, Taxes, and Other Illusions* by Arnold Patent. For many people, taxes are an annoying fact of life. Yet higher wisdom calls us to question what we have been told are the facts of life.

There are several ways to get free of the emotional burden of taxes. The first is to realize, as Jesus explained to Peter, that the children of a king do not pay taxes. In all of Jesus's parables, the king represents God. Because you are a child of God, everything in the kingdom is already yours. Why would you pay taxes to a kingdom you already own and rule? When you know that you are spiritual royalty, you don't pay royalties to anyone. The universe delights in providing for all your needs.

If you have ever flown internationally, you have seen flight attendants rolling carts through the aisles, selling duty-free items. Because the aircraft is in the air above the Earth, and not in any particular country, you are not subject to the taxes of the country you departed from, or the one you are headed to. When you elevate your consciousness above the Earth and establish yourself in the mindset of heaven, you are not subject to the rules that people make in the nations far below.

In a heavenly economy, there is no sense of burden, obligation, or oppression by a force outside of ourselves. Everyone does what they love, and everything gets done. The divine economy is joy-based, not fear-based. People contribute to the community because they are happy to do so, and there are no laws that force people to give what they do not wish to give or do what they do not wish to do. There are no wars, greed, or mismanagement of funds that drain the community bank. Well-being is the only reality. Your higher self has never paid taxes, and it never will. It exists in a reality that far transcends the domain that Caesar rules. The more you see yourself as tax-free, the more you can generate the experience of being tax-free.

You can also transcend a tax burden by expanding your consciousness so you generate enough financial prosperity that you can pay your taxes without feeling like you are losing. You can contribute to the government, and still have plenty of money to do all the things you want and need to do. Think of the good things the government is doing with your contribution, and the people you are helping. When you drop resistance to taxes, they retreat to a minor part of your psyche and your experience.

When a student told a spiritual teacher that she did not want to pay the amount of taxes she was asked to pay, he asked her, "Why do you tax yourself?" This is the intrapersonal teaching about how to address taxation. Everything that an external person or organization seems to be doing to us, we do to ourselves. If you feel burdened by government taxes, you are really taxing yourself. The government is simply playing out your belief. Do you believe that you must surrender a large portion of your good to an entity that has power over you? Do you harbor a belief in sacrifice and victimization? Are you capable of generating unlimited income, or are you restricted to what the world tells you that you can get? Answering these questions transforms the process of paying taxes into a powerful spiritual seminar. When you recognize that you are at choice about your experience, you achieve a huge step in spiritual awakening.

Through many of his parables and conversations, Jesus was training us to escape the fear and struggle we have learned to associate with money. Finances, like all elements of the material world, are meant to be a positive symbol of the presence and love of God. Every time you receive or spend money, you are participating in divine circulation. Jesus Christ does not want you to feel taxed, emotionally or financially. He wants you to know that you always have enough of everything you need. Then you can move from your assumed residence in a foreign land, and your false identity as someone who owes, to your rightful home in the palace and your true identity as a rich and royal soul.

PEARLS BEFORE PIGS

While sitting in a high school faculty room, I overheard a teacher telling a small group of her peers about a hair-raising experience she had had the previous weekend. "My husband and I went ice fishing last weekend. I fell through some thin ice, and nearly drowned. When my husband finally pulled me out, I thought I would freeze to death. I have never been so scared!"

Hearing that, another teacher commented, "Yes, it was pretty cold last weekend." The teacher who told the story sat there, stunned. The other teacher missed the entire point of the story.

Have you ever told anyone about a meaningful experience you had, and they looked at you like you were speaking Martian? Or they doubted and argued with you? Or they changed the subject, invalidating what you just said? Or they tried to top your story with a better one of their own? If so, you know how disheartening it can be to try to explain a personally sensitive moment to someone who is not ready or able to hear it.

After Jesus healed a man with a bad skin disease, he instructed him, "Do not tell anyone about this." Here again we learn from Jesus the master psychologist. If you experience a healing or epiphany, that event is tender within you, like a baby in a womb. If you speak of your experience before the lesson is solidified, others who do not understand or who doubt it may throw cold water over your hot experience and undermine the gift you received. You must protect your inner visions from unhealthy influences. Later, when your knowing is more firmly established, you can tell anyone, and you will help people by sharing your experience. Until then, you do better to tell no one, or perhaps tell just one or a few people you know will support and encourage you.

> Do not give dogs what is sacred; do not throw your
> pearls to pigs. If you do, they may trample them
> under their feet, and turn and tear you to pieces.

If you speak indiscriminately to an unreceptive person, you might feel stupid or intimidated, and wish you had never opened your mouth. That person may twist what you told them and attempt to use the information to demean you. They may cite evidence to the contrary. You may start to doubt what felt real when it happened. Jesus was trying to preempt such misuse and discouragement by advising to keep your lips sealed. Everything that happens to you is not for everyone to hear. It is for the right people who will accept and support you, and help you build your vision rather than tear it down.

Fear Feels Threatened by Love

Why would someone cast doubt or argue with someone who has had a positive experience? Simply, many people are afraid of love. Because the world of fear depends on darkness to keep its illusions in force, someone who brings light poses a threat. Many people have an investment in drama, negativity, sickness, limitation, and dysfunction, so when an individual comes along who has stepped into a brighter, freer world, the dysfunctional person has to knock that happy person down in order to edify their sorrowful position. If this dynamic sounds crazy, it is. The world does not rally around people who rise above a victim mentality and claim well-being. Misery doesn't just love company; it works overtime to keep unhappy people in its camp.

Regroup and Triumph

If you do cast pearls before a pig and your treasure gets trampled, you can make the experience work on your behalf. Negative or frustrating experiences can stimulate valuable course corrections. Here are some tips on how to deal with people who attempt to shred your joy:

1. Note that this person is not on your top ten list of people to discuss your intimate experiences. Keep future conversations lighter, or don't spend a lot of time with this person.

2. The moment you sense pushback, stop. Say no more. Change the subject.

3. Never try to convince the other person or argue with them until they understand or agree with you. The more you

debate, the deeper the hole you will dig. "Never wrestle with a pig. You both get dirty, and the pig likes it."

4. Validate yourself by recognizing that your experience is real and important, regardless of who understands it, or doesn't.

5. Consider why you give your power away to other people and let their reactions determine your happiness. Why do you need their understanding, agreement, or approval? If, as a result of dealing with their resistance, you are less likely to let your happiness depend on the reactions of others, you have made the event work in your favor.

6. Find compassion for the other person. What pain or struggle are they dealing with that makes them so insensitive? Have they been wounded and become cynical? People enmeshed in suffering cannot appreciate the good that befalls others.

7. Find other people who are safe to share your intimate story with. There are individuals and groups who value your inner life and support you to express what is important to you. They celebrate your triumphs rather than try to defeat you.

Protect Your Meal

Metaphysically, Jesus was not referring to other people as pigs, although many people display pig behaviors. The real pig is the hypercritical intellect that seeks to tear to shreds anything it does not understand or finds threatening. It is not simply a person before whom you must not cast pearls, but the *swine mind* that grunts in your head, and that of others. You are in charge of the voices in your head, and you must keep your thoughts in alignment with well-being.

On the Hawaiian island of Kauai, there is an overpopulation of wild chickens. Clucking hens and crowing roosters are everywhere—in parks, shopping centers, gas stations, and backyards. When I dined at an island restaurant with outdoor seating, chickens roamed the grounds looking for food. Some of the chickens are aggressive and jump onto the tabletops while customers are dining. To combat the intruders, the restaurant owner has placed small spray bottles of water on the tables for patrons to squirt the chickens who attempt to get to their meal. The owner, with a good sense of humor, has placed a sign on each table with instructions in large bold letters:

**"TAKE ANY AND ALL MEANS NECESSARY
TO PROTECT YOUR FOOD!"**

I found this missive a good metaphor for keeping unbridled intruders from devouring the uplifting thoughts in our mind. We cannot afford to allow destructive ideas to gobble up what makes us happy and improves our lives. We are much too tolerant of mind wandering and dark imaginings. When a problem arises, you might indulge in catastrophic fantasies. If so, remember the restaurant's sign to take any and all means necessary to protect the thoughts that empower you. You would never put up with a chicken jumping onto your table to eat your meal, so why would you allow fear-based thoughts to devour your blessings?

The part of your mind that doubts, criticizes, and overanalyzes has never obtained for you the peace you yearn for, and it never will. "Your ego is not your amigo." Your real amigo is your higher mind that cannot be touched or hurt by your own swine mind or that of others. If you have decommissioned your inner swine, negativity from other people cannot disturb you. Take refuge in the mind that God gave you rather than the one the world has laid upon you. Then you will emerge triumphant and walk through life unsullied and empowered.

The Pearl of Great Price

Jesus also spoke of a pearl when he described heaven as "the pearl of great price." When you have something you really value, your first priority is to take good care of it. Let nothing in the world steal your experience of heaven. In many ways the world is designed to distract you from heaven and replace it with lesser treasures. A true spiritual master is vigilant to keep the main thing the main thing.

You are not selfish to guard your soul. The more peace you carry within you, the more peace you bring to the world. Reserve your precious conversations for people who share your vision. When you retain your inner peace, you are in the best position to help other people get free of their own swine mind. As you model a mind established in light, you maximize the opportunity for those who look upon you to step into the light themselves. Take any and all means necessary to protect the spiritual banquet before you, and no wild pig or chicken will remove your blessings.

Get Out of My Father's House

When Jesus arrived in Jerusalem for Passover, he went to visit the great temple. There he was appalled to find a huge commercial enterprise dominating the scene. Merchants were selling all kinds of animals for sacrifices, and changing Greek and Roman currency for local shekels.

> He cast out all who sold and bought in the temple, and overthrew the tables of the money changers, and the seats of those who sold doves. He said to them, "It is written, 'My house shall be called the house of prayer'; but you have made it a den of thieves!"

It's easy to imagine people preoccupied with money infiltrating the religion of Jesus's time; we are all too aware of the same trapping today. After a prophet or visionary has established a religion or organization with noble purpose, greedy people often penetrate the institution, and the ministry becomes a business. Missions that started out with pure intent drift to worship at the altar of the dollar, and formerly pure endeavors become muddied. The congregation becomes ensnared in raising funds rather than consciousness, and church decisions revolve around income rather than inspiration.

We can't fault religious or spiritual groups for fundraising. Church activities require financial support; we live in a world where money is required to do anything material. Building or sustaining a church is expensive, and money must change hands. Even Jesus's ministry transacted finances; we are told that Judas was the treasurer for the master and his apostles.

Jesus objected to the massive mall scene in the temple because people had allowed materialism to replace their spiritual life. While the Bible does not say so specifically, I wonder if Jesus was also rejecting the practice of making blood sacrifices. The predominant sales at the temple were doves and other animals to be sacrificed on the altar—a barbaric practice. I cannot imagine that Jesus, a proponent of nonviolence, was pleased with the murder of animals to appease God. Perhaps one of his messages in driving trade out of the temple was you don't have to kill to make God happy.

Was Jesus Angry?

The story of Jesus lashing out at the temple merchants raises a key question: Was Jesus angry? If so, does this behavior run counter to his teaching to love thy neighbor as thyself, turn the other cheek, be as clever as serpents but gentle as doves, and forgive seventy times seven? One of the gospels tells that Jesus took a whip and slashed the tables of the vendors. Such a violent vendetta certainly doesn't seem characteristic of the Prince of Peace.

Some theologians argue that Jesus wasn't really angry. He was making a dramatic statement to teach a strong lesson. He wanted to get everyone's attention to learn that capitalism should not overtake religion. Are we simply projecting our own anger onto an innocent educational act?

On the other hand, is it possible that Jesus, while generally retaining his identity as the son of God, also had his human moments? Were there situations where he allowed emotion to overtake him? Was Jesus perfect all the time, or did he walk the same path we all do, sometimes remembering our true self, and at other times forgetting? Can the incident inspire us to have compassion for ourselves when we do not act perfectly godly?

One thing is for sure: Jesus Christ could not simultaneously be God and be angry. Anger is a human experience that God does not know, a projection of humanity onto divinity. Voltaire said, "If God has created us in His image, we have returned the favor." Considering that anger is fear under pressure, if God as Jesus became angry, God must have been afraid—an impossible situation.

Either Jesus momentarily lost his cool, or he exhibited apparently violent behavior without being upset. What do you think?

The Dark Twist

While we might interpret Jesus's purging the temple as anger-free, some theologians have twisted the story to justify violence in the name of Christ. They use the incident to rationalize crusades, inquisitions, the murder of infidels, lynchings, witch burnings, racism, and genocide. Here we behold Satan's greatest triumph, preempting Christ as head of the church. "If Jesus beat people into submission, so can we."

Yet Jesus Christ had nothing to do with violence; everything he stood for denies anyone's right to purposely inflict pain on another human being. His life and teachings were about kindness, mercy, and forgiveness. He devoted his ministry to inspire us to reach to attain these noble traits. Practicing these divine attributes, rather than punishment and retaliation, affords us our only chance to make Earth more like heaven. Those who justify heinous acts in the name of Christ have fallen prey to the harshest of illusions and shrouded light in a cloak of unspeakable darkness.

Cleansing the Inner Temple

To benefit most from the story, we must once again recognize that all the elements and characters in the scenario live *within* us. The great temple represents the holy sanctuary where God dwells in our heart, the quiet soul space that gives us entrée to the divine. The money changers and merchants reflect the part of our mind that is distracted by material pursuits to the point that we lose our inner peace. Jesus represents our true self, the healing voice calling us to live in alignment with our divine nature.

Imagine you owned a business in which you hired someone who promised to help you, but who is actually undermining you. While this person brags that he is earning you greater profits, he is stealing large sums from your bank account. He is also covertly attempting to rally other workers to sabotage your success. If you discovered the disastrous effect this person was perpetrating, you would surely fire him. You would do everything in your power to get rid of him and keep him from damaging your business any more.

The ego promises to bring us peace, but secretly distances us from it. It represents itself as our savior while it is really a saboteur. Daily we are misled by false beliefs that siphon off our joy. But the Christ in us will not put up with self-defeating attitudes and behaviors. It drives out what puts your well-being in danger. The Christ voice tells the inner saboteur, "Get out of my Father's house!" Your mind is a sacred place; no interlopers should be allowed to undermine your happiness. All negative thinking must be banished so you can invest your energy in far more rewarding ventures.

Your inner Christ does not need to whip the ego to banish it from the temple. It simply shines the light of truth so brightly that the dysfunctional elements of your psyche dissolve. It is tempting to wage war against darkness; yet war *is* darkness. You cannot end war with a war on war. More darkness will not displace the night; only the light will bring dawn. When Jesus called us to "be the light of the world" and "return evil with good," he was giving us the formula to purge the thieves from our sacred inner sanctuary.

Wield St. Michael's Sword

Artists and sculptors depict the archangel St. Michael as wielding a long, sharp, gleaming sword. This weapon symbolizes our power to slice illusions away from reality. It is the tool of divine discernment. Every day presents us with many opportunities to choose between truth and lies; to decide if we will indulge in fear or make a stand for love. St. Michael's sword is not a weapon to pierce a body, but rather to cut away all that does not serve us, and preserve what heals us. St. Michael is not a murderer. He is a liberator.

Politicians warn us of "weapons of mass destruction." Jesus warns us of weapons of mass distraction. We spend too much of our life pursuing things that do not take us where we really want to go. How much more powerful we are when we stay focused on the divine presence! In getting rid of the merchants who occupied the temple, Jesus was wielding the sword of St. Michael. So must we all do when we are confronted with interlopers who clog the entrance to great temple of our spirit.

The house of prayer is our refuge from an insane world. We will not find peace selling or making sacrifices. Prayer is far more than muttering a rote script; Jesus warned us against vain repetition. When you feel joyful, you are lighting the temple and fulfilling its purpose and yours. A happy person brings God to the world far more effectively than a miserable one. Let us remove the saboteurs of anger, depression, despair, materialism, and greed from our inner cathedral. We drive them out not with whips, but by replacing them with gratitude, reverence for the holy presence, and celebration. This is how we restore the temple of truth to its original glory.

Just Say the Word

A Roman centurion came to Jesus and pleaded, "Lord, my servant lies at home paralyzed, suffering terribly."

Jesus asked, "Would you like me to come and heal him?"

The centurion replied, "Lord, I do not deserve to have you come under my roof. But just say the word. For I myself am a man under authority, with soldiers under me. I tell this one, 'Go,' and he goes; and that one, 'Come,' and he comes. I say to my servant, 'Do this,' and he does it."

When Jesus heard this, he was amazed and said to the crowd following him, "Truly I tell you, I have not found anyone in Israel with such great faith . . ."

Then Jesus said to the centurion, "Go! Let it be done just as you believed it would."

His servant was healed at that very hour.

Our words can make or break our life. What comes out of our mouth returns to us in the form of tangible events. The same power of the word that Jesus used to heal the centurion's servant is available to us. When you recognize the creative potential of the words you utter, you take care to speak only things that you wish to see come about.

"In the beginning was the word" does not apply only to the beginning of the universe. It applies to every word you speak. Every event and experience begins with a word. Thoughts are more subtle forms of words. So we can say with equal authority, "In the beginning was the thought."

The Power of "I Am"

The two most powerful words you can speak are, "I am." We must be extremely attentive to the words we utter after "I am." What you fill in that blank with tends to come true. What you say today is a coming attraction of the movie of your life you will see tomorrow.

"I am" defines the identity you claim. In truth, you have only one identity—God—and nothing you say or do can change who you are. But because God has imbued us with the power to create with our mind, we can produce experiences contrary to the divine. You can make up a pitiful story and live in it as if it is true, even while you are a glorious, triumphant soul. If you say, "I am sick," or "I am depressed," or "I am poor," you are telling a lie.

Then you reinforce and perpetuate the experience the lie generates. When you speak the truth, "I am well"; "I am wealthy"; or "I am loved," you strengthen and expand those experiences.

The prophet Joel said, "Let the weak say, 'I am strong.'" Behind and beneath our belief in weakness lives a deeper, stronger self. Everything God is, we are. Everything God is not, we are not. Only the attributes of God befit us; all else is an error in perception. God cannot be weak, so neither can you. Joel was calling us to shift our self-perception from frailty to mastery.

The metaphysical master Florence Scovel Shinn based her entire ministry on the power of the word. People seeking physical healing, rewarding relationships, and expanded prosperity came to Ms. Shinn to speak the word for them. As a result, they enjoyed remarkable manifestations and miracles. She wrote a book titled, *Your Word is Your Wand,* indicating that we have the power to generate heaven or hell, health or illness, riches or poverty, by the words we speak.

Most people do not realize the power of their words, so they misuse their vocabulary and create and prolong situations that hurt them. But they hurt themselves first with thoughts and words that run contrary to the well-being they desire and deserve. When you consciously activate the power of your words, you become a healer and an uplifter. Never underestimate the influence of your words. The more you speak your good, the more your good will find you.

Cast the Devils Out of Your Mind

In some of his healings, Jesus laid hands on people. With others, he simply spoke the word. Words extend our healing power far beyond our fingertips. Hands move in the dimension of the flesh. Words move in the dimension of the mind. Since mind is the field in which we live, not limited by time or distance, words spread healing beyond the metrics of touch.

The Bible tells us that Jesus cast out devils. When he encountered people who were possessed, Jesus boldly commanded, "Satan, get out!" and the person was released. We can account for such healing in scientific terms. Every word we think or speak rings with a specific vibration. Fear, negativity, and disease function at a low, dense vibration. Love, positivity, and healing function at a lighter, higher frequency. When you apply a high vibration to a low vibration situation, the situation transforms. When Jesus commanded, "Satan, get out!" he was mobilizing the power of the word to replace dark energy with light. When illusions meet truth, truth prevails. Nothing unreal can continue to exist in the presence of the real.

You will not get rid of negative thoughts by fighting them; resistance only empowers them. What you resist, expands and persists. The way to heal negative thoughts is to replace them with positive ones. When you notice negation arising, find the thoughts that represent their healing alternative, and dwell on them. Thus you are casting the devils out of your mind.

Why Jesus Would Visit Your House

The centurion's statement, "I do not deserve for you to enter my house" represents a feeling of unworthiness that many of us harbor. We have been trained to believe that we are sinful or deficient, and God would not waste His time trying to help us. Or we deserve to be punished, and we must pay off our negative karma before we merit healing. The centurion's adverse self-valuation ran counter to Jesus's ministry, for the mystical messiah was famous—and criticized—for hanging out with disrespected people and lost souls. He declared, "I will go wherever I am welcome." While Jesus would have entered the centurion's home, the soldier did not believe he would come, so the man did not invite him. Yet Jesus found a workaround, and sent his word to heal the servant.

While you may have judgments about foolish errors you have made, your shameful past, or people you have hurt, Jesus does not share such perceptions of you. All he sees is a shining soul reaching for healing. Guilt, an invention of the deluded human ego, is not an element in Christ's mental repertoire. He would gladly enter your home if you invited him. If you are reading this book, he already has. Metaphysically, your home represents your mind. Jesus will happily enter your mind and heal your painful thoughts if you allow him.

Jesus's willingness to help the centurion also provides a model for us to drop our judgments when others come to us for help. If Jesus could dine with pompous priests and help a Roman soldier's servant, you can overlook your husband slurping his soup. Remember that every human action is either a pure expression of love or a call for love. When we reframe meanspirited or foolish actions as a call for love, we can cross the bridge over the river of judgment and replace alienation with resolution.

Just as You Believed

Jesus's statement, "Let it be done just as you believed it would" yields another crucial teaching. The master was crediting the centurion's belief as the door through which healing was delivered. The soldier's respect for the power of the word led him to trust that Jesus's word would achieve the healing, and it did.

Belief is a major element in healing or any form of success. Jesus was affirming the power of intention to create experience. He had disciplined his mind to align with well-being, so when he spoke the word, healing was accomplished. You and I can achieve the same success when we bring our thoughts into alignment with higher truth. Then the power of the entire universe is behind us.

Jesus also healed a man who had been blind since birth. The master spat on a clump of dirt, turned it into mud, and rubbed it on the man's eyes. Immediately his sight was restored. Was there some magic in the dirt muddied by Jesus's spittle? Not at all. The mud was a permission slip onto which the blind man and observers projected their faith. Mud has no power, even if Jesus Christ spits into it. All power is in belief. If Jesus had simply spoken the word, the recipient would not have had enough belief to push the miracle over the edge to manifestation. But a three-dimensional object seemed real enough to get the job done.

Do You Want to be Healed?

In Jerusalem Jesus came upon a man who had been paralyzed for thirty-eight years. He was lying beside the Pool of Bethesda, where people believed that if you were the first one in the pool when the waters were stirred, you would get healed. Jesus asked the invalid, "Do you want to get healed?" The man replied, "I have no one to take me in the waters when they are stirred." Jesus replied, "Get up, take up your mat, and walk." In that moment the man was healed. He took up his mat, and walked.

Several elements of this story are highly relevant for all of us. First, people were superstitious about needing to be the first one in the water in order to be healed. The paralyzed man fell into this superstition and blamed others for not taking him in the water as the reason he remained disabled. He misattributed his power to water and people, neither of which are the source of healing. The mind aligned with truth is the source of healing.

But Jesus's intention for the man to be healed superseded superstition and complaint. The mat Jesus called the man to take up was not the straw remnant he slept on, but the limiting beliefs with which he had become entrenched. He had become lazy in his mind, stuck in a rut of constricting self-definition.

When Jesus asked him, "Do you want to be healed?" he confronted the man with the choice he had been avoiding. The fellow accepted Jesus's challenge, picked up his old beliefs, and took them away from his entrenched position.

I observe this dynamic in some of my coaching clients. One fellow had been diagnosed with ADHD. "I don't think I am totally ADHD," he told me. "I can focus and get things done if I want to."

"Then why don't you focus all the time?" I asked him.

"I am afraid that if I get my projects done and show them to the world, I will be criticized. So it's easier to stay ADHD, not finish my projects, and avoid the judgment I fear."

Another client complained that she was a chronic pro-crastinator and never got around to cleaning her house. "Why is procrastinating more rewarding to you than cleaning your house?" I asked.

"My father was a perfectionist and he demanded that I be the same," she told me. "I'm afraid that if I do my task and it's not perfect, I will feel like a failure."

In both cases, these people had gotten comfortable on their mat of limiting beliefs. They needed to pick up their old negative programs, rise out of them, and move forward.

The Bible story applies to any of us who have gotten so steeped in old patterns that we perceive more reward in maintaining them than changing. We may also blame others for not doing for us what we can do for ourselves. When our higher self, represented by Jesus, commands us to get out of our rut and get moving, his authority breaks up solidified patterns, and the healing we thought was impossible happens.

The Power of Subconscious Intention

There are words even more powerful than the words we speak with our lips. These are the words we speak in our subconscious. Freud was correct when he described the mind as an iceberg with a tiny part visible and the greater part below the surface of our awareness. Some scientists estimate that ninety-five percent of mental activity occurs on the subconscious level. The subconscious does not speak words. It holds ideas, which are words in a more essential state. While you create your life by the words you speak, you more fundamentally create your life by the ideas you hold.

My client Haley posed this situation: "My mother was a lifelong hypochondriac. She spent a great deal of her life complaining and visiting doctors, who found little wrong with her.

She ultimately lived a long life and died at age ninety-two. If the words we speak determine our experience, and my mother spoke constantly of her ill health, how did she stay healthy and live so long?"

I explained to Haley, "Your mother enjoyed the attention she got from complaining about her imaginary diseases. This attention was life-giving to her. The reward she perceived from the sympathy she received outweighed the problems she complained about. Regardless of what her conscious mind and words were saying, she subconsciously intended to live for a long time, and so she did."

You can always tell what you believe by what you are getting. We can use outer events as a mirror to help us become aware of our inner choices.

Closer to God than the Masses

When Jesus heard the words of the centurion and told the people around him, "This man has greater faith than anyone I have found in Israel," he was teaching that religious practices are not the same as faith. While the Jewish people were pious religiously, they were in many ways hollow of faith. Here came a Roman, considered a godless pagan, and his faith in healing was perfect.

Spiritual empowerment has a little to do with outer actions, and a lot to do with state of mind. You can spend a lifetime performing righteous acts, and still suffer from a sense of separation from God. The workings of the inner mind run much deeper than religious beliefs. My friend Don calls himself an atheist. Yet he is one of the kindest, most sincere, and most honorable people I have ever known. He is a devoted husband

and father, and enjoys loving relationships with his children. When I put my house on the market, Don purchased it, and his generosity and integrity in the transaction were impeccable. Regardless of his lack of religious affiliation, he has a golden heart and his presence in the world is a blessing. What Don calls himself doesn't matter. How he lives, does.

While we often interchange the words "religion" and "faith," they are not necessarily the same thing. Your experience of life is not based on your religion. It is based on what you believe in. We all have faith in something. Some people have faith in God, and others have faith in money. Some have faith in cooperation, and others have faith in competition. Some have faith in Jesus, others Allah, others Buddha, and others, artistic expression. I saw a YouTube video showing an early Beatles performance. A viewer who called himself an atheist commented, "If ever there was proof of God, it is the talent by which the Beatles brought so much joy and upliftment to the world." Even an atheist was seeking some proof of God, and he found it.

Everyone finds healing through their own chosen avenue. One route is not better or more valuable than the others. The name of Christ is indeed powerful, yet the energy the word represents is universal, no matter the word that expresses it. When you heal in the name of love, you are healing in the name of Christ. The phrase "keep the faith" is apt, not because it refers to the power of religion, but because of the power of faith. When you speak the word with faith, the universe is at your command.

COME FORTH!

Of all the miracles Jesus performed, raising Lazarus from the dead is the most dramatic. It's one thing to restore a sick person to health, but bringing a deceased person back to life is quite another. Lazarus is not the only resurrection Jesus achieved. He also raised the son of the widow of Nain, as well as the daughter of Jairus. He later went on to return after his own crucifixion.

While it's exciting to recount these spectacular stories, let's delve into the dynamics of how Jesus achieved such miracles, and—even more important—how you and I can restore vitality to dead elements of our life, and help others do the same.

Lazarus and his sisters Mary and Martha were beloved friends of Jesus. When Lazarus fell gravely ill, his sisters sent a message to Jesus asking him to come to Bethany and heal him. Upon hearing the news, Jesus wept. He waited two days, and then made his way to Lazarus's home.

By the time Jesus arrived, Lazarus had died and he had already been entombed for four days. Martha met Jesus and complained, "If you had come sooner, you could have saved my brother."

Jesus approached the tomb and asked the observers to roll away the stone covering the entrance. He knelt and prayed, "Thank you, Father, for answering my prayer." Then he boldly commanded, "Lazarus, come forth!" Moments later, to everyone's astonishment, Lazarus emerged from the tomb clad in his burial clothes. Jesus told the people to remove the garments, and the man went on with his life.

This stirring scenario is filled with symbolic teachings. First, we must note that when Jesus learned that Lazarus was dying, he wept. Here again we see that Jesus shared the human experience we all walk through. While the master was one with God, he also felt the emotions that touch our lives. Most depictions of Christ cast him as the one who walked on water, not the one who tramped through mud, as we all do. Saddened at the imminent loss of his friend, he showed his sorrow. "Jesus wept" is the shortest sentence in the entire Bible, indicating that the master spent a little time weeping, and the great majority of his time healing. This passage gives us permission to be human, and then to dwell in the presence of God beyond our tenderness.

Martha's complaint that Jesus arrived too late typifies a lack of faith we all slip into. "If only that would have happened (or not happened), my life would be much better." Yet even while we protest some fault in the divine plan, there is no interruption in providence. *A Course in Miracles* tells us, "All things work together for good. There are no exceptions except in the ego's judgment." In the moment of her upset, Martha fell into ego.

Should you become impatient or regretful, practice the affirmation, "God's timing is perfect." All things unfold in perfect sequence. If we believe in timing mistakes, we have laid our demand of when things should happen over when they do best to happen. If you can relax and trust divine order, the natural order reveals itself, and the ego is humbled in the face of a greater, wiser plan.

Don't Waste Time Explaining

Jesus did not make any response to Martha's criticism. He simply went about the business of resurrecting her brother. When you follow higher guidance, you do not need to apologize, argue, justify, or explain—all wastes of time for a spiritual master. You simply get on with the task at hand and trust that people who don't understand or who are upset will figure it out when things work out well anyway.

It is said, "People who don't believe in you won't hear any explanation, and people who believe in you don't need any explanation." The more you try to justify, the deeper the hole you dig. Don't even start. "When your work speaks for itself, don't interrupt."

Roll Away the Stone

Jesus's command, "Roll away the stone" is a key metaphor. Whenever we perceive an insurmountable problem or an irretrievable loss, we have let the stone of small thinking block our vision of greater possibilities. The real stone is the belief in limitation. Before we can see a solution, we have to roll aside dark beliefs and daunting expectations. Then the thing that seems dead, buried, unhealable, or impossible can step forth into the light and thrive in full splendor.

The Answered Prayer

Jesus delivered a compelling model when he thanked his Father for answering his prayer even before he saw its manifestation. This is consistent with Jesus's teaching that our request has already been granted. ("Behold, the field is ripe for harvest now.") This is how we should pray. Rather than asking God for something we hope will happen, and then reserving our thanks until after we see the result, we must enter into the gratitude state of mind in which the gift has already been given. We must proceed *from* the result rather than toward it.

During the past few decades, a new field called "vision psychology" has emerged. Practitioners teach the technique of picturing our goals so clearly in our mind that we feel we already have achieved them. When a star basketball player was asked, "How do you score so many points?" he answered, "The ball is in the basket before it leaves my hand." Jesus demonstrated this dynamic two thousand years ago. Psychology is gradually catching up with the universal principles Jesus revealed. Ultimately what human beings learn through science will corroborate spiritual truths that have been known and taught for millennia.

Come Forth!

The paramount teaching in Jesus raising Lazarus was the master's command, "Lazarus, come forth!" To whom was Jesus speaking? Certainly not to the decaying corpse. Jesus pierced beyond the physical appearance into the spiritual reality. He knew that the soul of the man called Lazarus was very much alive and fully intact, regardless of his apparent material condition. Jesus taught, "Judge not by appearances, but judge by righteous judgment." In other words, "Don't be fooled by what the physical senses show you." While Lazarus's sisters were steeped in mourning, Jesus was established in morning. He paid no attention to the limiting form, but gave full attention to the living spirit, which responded and emerged whole and triumphant.

To be an effective healer, teacher, parent, or leader, you must establish yourself in the highest vision of your clients, students, children, or team. People live up to your expectations, or down to your criticism. You generate results by focusing on what you want rather than resisting what you don't want. Define yourself by what you are for, not what you are against; by what you want to become, not what you fear you or others are. I used to see a chiropractor who would greet me, "How is the healthiest guy on the planet today?" I didn't think of myself as the healthiest guy on the planet, but when he called me that, I definitely felt healthier. He was commanding my well-being, "Come forth!" and it did.

Likewise, you can call forth your students' best grades, your patients' healing, your family's harmonious relationships, or your corporate team's record-breaking sales. Universal principles work wherever we apply them. Jesus was not imbued with any special powers we do not all share. He did not come to set himself apart from humanity, but to call us to achieve the mastery he demonstrated.

Your Personal Resurrection

Is there a part of you or your life that seems to have died? Have you lost your passion? Do you drag yourself through your days, wondering why you are here? Do you believe that your best years are behind you? Have you experienced so much pain in relationships that you have sealed your heart in a tomb of protection? Have you become so serious that you cannot laugh? Have you lost faith that humanity can overcome the challenges we face?

If so, it's time to roll back the stone and command your highest and truest self, "Come forth!" When Jairus and his wife told Jesus that their daughter was dead, Jesus replied, "The girl is not dead. She is just sleeping." Jesus spoke a few words to the girl, and she rose. Likewise, the parts of your life that seem dead are just sleeping. Like Lazarus, your Christed self is calling you to emerge from your tomb and remove the grave clothes; they are not appropriate attire for the party to which you are invited. Lazarus went on with his new life, as did Jairus's daughter, and so will you. The spiritual gifts you embody cannot die because they have been placed there by God. As you emerge from the crypt of fear and daunting history, you stand in full daylight, and you are ready to get on with the best part of your journey. Death in any form is no obstacle to a living spirit. Command your highest life, "Come forth!" and it surely will.

24

MOVING THE
IMMOVABLE JUDGE

Jesus raising Lazarus was not the result of the suspension of universal laws. It was the result of intelligent application of principles that always work on our behalf when we dispatch them with faith and intention. The master told a fascinating parable that reveals how we can use those laws to our advantage when we understand the interaction between focused thinking and manifestation:

In a certain town there was a judge who did not fear God or care about people. A widow in that town kept coming to the judge and pleading, "Grant me justice against my adversary."

For a long time the judge refused. But eventually he said to himself, "Even though I do not fear God or care about people, this widow keeps annoying me, so I will see that she gets justice. That way she will not wear me down by her continually beseeching me."

Listen to the response of the unjust judge. Will not God deliver justice to his chosen ones, who cry out to him day and night? Will he keep putting them off? I tell you, he will see that they get justice, and quickly.

This parable is usually understood as a teaching to be persistent in prayer. If you pray hard enough and long enough, God will answer your prayer. Good advice. Yet the intrapersonal lesson runs far deeper.

The unjust judge in this story represents subconscious beliefs you hold that work against you. The judge does not care about God or people, meaning that the Law of Mind is impersonal. ("God is no respecter of persons.") Universal laws will serve you or hamper you, depending on how you use them. Subconscious self-defeating beliefs are unkind and unfair to you because you deserve the justice of God's love. You are not battling an authority outside you. Your real opponents are the judgmental thoughts you hold in your mind. Only self-doubt and guilt can prevent you from having the good things you deserve.

Yet the widow refused to accept the judge's initial rejection, meaning that you are not bound by your subconscious programming. Even if you have carried limiting beliefs for many years, they can be replaced with self-honoring beliefs that yield you God's blessings. But you must be persistent in addressing and dismantling the negative thought patterns.

You achieve this victory through prayer, affirmation, visualization, or any other spiritual practice that elevates your consciousness. When you pray sincerely, speak an affirmation consistently, or visualize with feeling, you chip away at the limiting belief, and eventually it will dissolve. You are not dealing with a human or supernatural adversary. You are dealing with a habit of thought. A negative belief is formed by erroneous thoughts you think over and over again. You can replace that belief by thinking new, truer thoughts over and over again. The widow continually returning to the judge represents you chiseling away at the wall of negative judgment until it crumbles. You can also think of a negative belief as a block of ice. When you keep tossing hot water on the ice, it will melt.

Overcoming an Unfair World

We all believe that we have been treated unfairly in some way. Some relative abused you as a child; kids at school bullied you; a lover or spouse betrayed you; someone less qualified than you got the promotion you wanted; you have been the victim of religious, cultural, or racial prejudice; you are economically disadvantaged; the government does not properly provide for you; or perhaps you carry a physical disability. There is no shortage of ways we have been hurt for no good reason.

Yet *A Course in Miracles* advises us, "Beware of the temptation to perceive yourself unfairly treated." It asks us to remember, "I am not the victim of the world I see." These teachings run counter to the world's agreement on injustice and victimization. How can we resolve injustice and get the unfair judge to render a fair verdict?

The key is to achieve a shift in perception. Cease to see yourself as the effect of other people's choices, and recognize that you create your life with your own choices. Let go of any victim identity, and claim mastery over your experience. These crucial transformations do not come overnight; they usually take time. If you give up after you do not get immediate results, you will not achieve your goal. Just as the widow kept banging on the judge's door, you must keep challenging the beliefs that hold you back. No one can stop you but yourself, and no one can advance you but yourself. God must have a great deal of faith in you to entrust you with the power of transformation. Now you must have the same faith in yourself.

Real Justice

To obtain justice, we must upgrade our understanding of justice. We have been trained to equate justice with punishment. But *A Course in Miracles* tells us that the only real justice is forgiveness. If you are going to demand justice, demand release from guilt, fear, indebtedness, and self-sabotage. The judge in the parable was unjust because he did not treat the widow kindly. Finally, he delivered justice by being as kind to the widow as she was to herself.

When the widow asked the judge to grant her justice against her adversary, we are prone to assume that her adversary is a person. While that may be true on the surface level of the story, the real adversary is self-defeating thinking, feeling, speaking, and living. It's tempting to think that we must fight some person or source outside of us. But enlightenment is an inside job. Conquering another person or organization is a lesser (and distracting) achievement compared to conquering our own sense of smallness. It seems easier to try to control the world than to control our mind. But because the world is in our mind, it is meaningless to control the outer world. The true triumph is internal.

Jesus concludes the parable by promising that when we persevere in asking God for justice, God will deliver it quickly. This is an interesting twist on the parable because the judge did not answer the widow's request immediately; it was only when she wore him down over time that he came around.

Again we must drop into the intrapersonal level of the parable to glean its meaning. The moment you know you deserve happiness, it will come. The good you seek is lined up outside your door, waiting for you to accept it. My client Mary Lu had gone through a difficult marriage that ended in divorce. Over a period of ten years, she had gone on some dates, but none of those relationships clicked. She feared that she would repeat her painful marriage. Now she sincerely wanted to find a worthy life partner. In coaching, we came up with the affirmation, "I am open, willing, and ready to connect with a wonderful life partner." This affirmation resonated with her, and she continued to practice it.

A few weeks later, Mary Lu participated in one of my webinars. She looked fantastic, ten years younger. Amazingly, a pleasant-looking man sat beside her. She reported, "After practicing my affirmation, I joined an online dating site. There I met Chester. We swapped some texts, met for coffee, and then started dating. We both feel we have met our right partner." Chester shared Mary Lu's spiritual values and he cared about her a great deal. They went on to enjoy a deeply rewarding relationship.

Mary Lu and Chester are living examples of the "quickly" conclusion to the parable of transforming the unjust judge. The moment she was ready, Mary Lu's miracle happened. When you are ready, so will yours.

Even if you do not manifest a material result immediately, you can enjoy inner peace now. That is the best manifestation of all. When you make soul satisfaction your goal, everything in the outer world follows naturally. Instead of letting inner peace hinge on an outer condition, build your outer conditions on your state of mind. This is how spontaneous remissions and healings occur. While you have been waiting for God to deliver your blessings, God has been waiting for you to receive them. Your sincere "yes" opens the door to miracles.

Prayer Moves Mountains

Prayer is the greatest power at our disposal because it joins our mind with God's mind. In prayer, we align our will with God's, and we receive the good that God wants for us. We don't need to convince God to deliver our blessings; we need to convince ourselves to accept them. Theologian Philip Brooks put it succinctly: "Prayer is not the overcoming of God's reluctance, but the taking hold of God's willingness."

A student asked my mentor Hilda Charlton to help her achieve a healing. Hilda replied, "If I were you, I would pound the ethers until I got my result." "Pounding the ethers" is equivalent to the widow persevering to convince the judge.

"The ethers" means the psychic atmosphere in which your sub-conscious mind dwells.

> Whoever says to this mountain, "Go, throw yourself into the sea," and does not doubt in his heart, but believes that what he says will come to pass, it will be done for him. Therefore I tell you, whatever you ask in prayer, believe that you have received it, and it will be yours.

Just as the widow moved the mountain of the judge's resistance, when we pray, we gain the leverage to shift anything on Earth. (*A Course in Miracles* asks us to remember, "There is nothing my holiness cannot do.") No religion owns the patent on prayer. You can pray religious prayers, spiritual prayers, or any prayer you formulate from your own heart. Any positive, creative thought is a prayer. Sincerity of intent is the active ingredient in prayer.

The unjust judge is humanity thinking, and the persistent widow is God thinking. The thoughts of God supersede the thoughts of humanity until the thoughts of humanity become the thoughts of God. Then the verdict is delivered fairly, and justice is accomplished.

ARE YOU MAKING THE MOST OF YOUR TALENTS?

M anifesting our highest good is never about importing something from the outer world. It is about allowing the best of our inner world to flow forth in natural expression. At this very moment you bear within you everything you need to live your highest dreams. Your job is to trust your gifts and deliver them.

A wealthy man, about to leave on a journey, entrusted a portion of his assets to three of his servants. To one he gave five talents [coins of significant value], to another, two talents, and to another, one talent. When he later returned home, the master asked each servant to give an accounting of what he had done with the talents he had been given.

The first servant reported that he had invested his five talents and earned five talents in return. The second servant had also doubled his investment. The master was pleased, and told them, "Well done . . . You have been faithful over a few things, and I will make you ruler over many things."

The third servant, however, did not invest the money or gain a return. Because he was afraid of losing the money, he hid his one talent in the ground. Hearing this, the master grew angry, since the servant had not improved on the investment. The master then had the unproductive servant punished.

These fiscal talents serve as a metaphor for personal talents. God has invested in every person unique and precious gifts. You might be a talented artist, writer, teacher, or chef. You may be good at working with children, caring for animals, or financial planning. Perhaps you are a minister, healer, or yoga instructor. There is something you love to do, you do it well, and it helps people. Every soul has some special passion and skill bestowed by the universe.

The question is, what are you doing with the talents you have been given? Are you expressing them plentifully and watching them bear fruit and multiply? Or are you hiding them in fear of exposing yourself, being judged, or failing? Have you allowed hesitation or a sense of unworthiness to eclipse the blessings available to you and those you influence?

The results you get from how you handle your talents are similar to the results you get from how you handle your money. If you invest a sum of money wisely, it will harvest a return greater than itself. A bank will pay you interest, real estate will appreciate in value, and a smart stock market purchase will yield a dividend. Money grows only when it moves.

If you do not move your money, it will diminish in value. If you hide it under a mattress, bury it in your back yard, or let it sit in a safe deposit box, you will lose some of it. Inflation will make it worth less than it is now. The nature and purpose of money is to circulate and stimulate prosperity in everyone it touches.

Likewise, talents grow when you put them to use, and they atrophy when you deny them. "Use it or lose it" applies to talent as well as money and muscles. The Chinese system of healing is built on the flow of *chi*, or life force. Illness is a result of stagnation or congestion of chi. A Chinese healing practitioner will give you acupuncture, massage, or herbs, or prescribe exercise to get your chi moving. Circulation is the answer to physical disease, as it is to mental, emotional, financial, or relationship maladies.

Jesus was urging us to shine our gifts into life. You were born to deliver certain blessings to humanity. When you give them, you experience deep soul fulfillment and you make the world a better place. When you withhold your talents, your life feels empty and you wonder what you are doing here. The antidote to depression, boredom, and confusion is authentic self-expression.

Ruler over Many Things

The wealthy man in the parable rewarded his servants who had made good investments by promising to make them ruler over many things. Because they had done well with a little, he would give them a lot.

When you demonstrate integrity over a small sector of life, your influence will naturally expand. Don't worry if you start a business and you have a small number of customers, or if you teach a class of just a few students. If you give your heart to your project, it will grow. The inspiring movie *Brother Sun, Sister Moon* dramatizes the life of St. Francis, who, after a spiritual epiphany, took it upon himself to single-handedly restore a tiny church that had fallen into ruin. Daily he added a few stones to the broken walls. Some of his friends watched what he was doing, and joined him. When the building was completed, he held a modest church service, which grew and grew until it was burgeoning with joyful people. Today St. Francis is loved, respected, and emulated by many millions of people. Small beginnings beget greater ends.

Appreciate what you have before asking for more. Make the most of your current resources before you attempt to expand. Many businesses fail because they try to grow too quickly. They have not built a foundation by taking the best care of the customers they already have. When more customers come, they enter a diluted field, and they are disappointed. When, on the other hand, you do right by the people already in your field of influence, the universe will send you more. Everything in nature grows gradually and organically, cell by cell, step by step. Astonish your current customers or students with stellar service, and they will come back and bring their friends.

Stewards of the Great King

Some aspirants think that the best way to grow spiritually is to retreat from the world. This is true for certain phases and periods. Yet we more powerfully master spirituality on the interactions of daily life. It's easy to keep your peace in a cave or monastery. But to maintain a sterling consciousness in the marketplace is a greater achievement. When we stay connected to our spirit downtown, we gain the double blessing of inner peace and material success. This is the zone of mastery.

We are all stewards of the great King, who has entrusted us with tremendous resources and powers. God has invested everything God is, in us. It is said, "What we are is God's gift to us. What we make of ourselves is our gift to God." Regardless of how empty or disconnected from passion you feel, tremendous gifts to humanity live within you. Your talents may shrink to an ember, but they cannot be extinguished. At any moment you can fan the spark into a bonfire. It's time to dig your talents up from the dirt and let the world enjoy what God gave you to give.

MASTERY THROUGH HUMILITY

"Where are we going today?" I asked my Japanese sponsor as she poured me a cup of matcha tea on the bullet train hurtling from Tokyo to Nagoya. "This afternoon you are going to co-present a lecture with Mr. Wahei Takeda, one of the wealthiest and most influential men in the country," she replied. "He is known as 'the Warren Buffet of Japan.'"

A bit intimidated but mostly excited, an hour later we arrived at Mr. Takeda's home, where he guided me on a tour of a private museum he had constructed to honor the gods and renowned leaders of ancient Japan. I found Wahei-san to be an extraordinarily kind, humble, and childlike soul. Though I was a guest unknown to him, he treated me with utmost respect, as if I were a dignitary.

After our lecture, Wahei-san took me to dinner, where we sat on the floor at a low table, laughed, and he told me endearing stories. One of his successful business ventures is a cookie factory. "I ask all of my employees to maintain a spirit of deep gratitude," he told me. "When they wrap each cookie, they speak a sincere, prayerful *arigato*—'thank you.' This imbues a blessing in each cookie, so the recipient's spirit is filled as well as their tummy." He also told me, "Whenever one of my employees has a baby, I give the child a gold coin to start them off on an abundant life."

Even though Wahei-san (who has since passed on) enjoyed one of the noblest reputations in Japan—a country with the highest value on reputation—he remained entirely humble. His humility earned him not just phenomenal business success, but the greatest success of all—peace of mind.

The Lesser Becomes the Greater

When he noticed how the guests picked the places of honor at the table, he told them this parable: "When someone invites you to a wedding feast, do not take the place of honor, for a person more distinguished than you may have been invited. If so, the host will come and say to you, 'Give this person your seat.' Then, humiliated, you will have to take the least important place. But when you are invited, take the lowest place, so that when your host comes, he will say to you, 'Friend, move up to a better place.' Then you will be honored in the presence of all the other guests. For all those who exalt themselves will be humbled, and those who humble themselves will be exalted."

The Talmud cites a similar teaching:

> He who seeks reputation shall lose it.
> He who does not seek reputation shall gain it.

At my synagogue, my mentor Stuie strove to live the precepts of Judaism. He pointed me to an ancient passage: "When you make a donation to charity, give anonymously." Don't attempt to draw attention to yourself and puff up your ego as a generous giver. During the Jewish high holidays, the president of that temple would announce to the congregation the names of the donors to the synagogue, and the amounts they had given. Every year he announced that there was one person who had given anonymously. When I heard the announcement, I giggled because everyone knew that Stuie was the only member of the temple who followed the precept. I respected him for his effort to live up to the teachings.

> And when you pray, do not be like the hypocrites, for they love to pray standing in the synagogues and on the street corners to be seen by men. I tell you the truth, they have received their reward in full. When you pray, go into your room, close the door and pray to your Father, who is unseen. Then your Father, who sees what is done in secret, will reward you.

Bragging as a Call for Love

People who are starving for love find all kinds of ways to get attention. Those who brag or bully, for example, are insecure. They tout their own accolades because they don't think they are enough. In trying to convince others, they are trying to convince themselves. People who know they are enough do not need to prove they are enough, and they don't need validation from the outside world. They rest secure in authentic self-recognition. An insecure person can never gather enough accolades from the world. While they accumulate titles and add more and more letters after their name, there are only three letters they really need: GOD. Bragging is a call for self-knowledge. If you know you are whole, you don't need to import people and stuff from the outer world to make you whole. If you know you are loveable, you don't need someone to say, "I love you." If you know you are created in the image and likeness of a perfect God, you don't need to struggle to look like a movie star. I have seen photos of supermodels without makeup, and they look quite normal. So if you are sweating to copy your idol, you are chasing an illusion. Rest in the natural beauty you already own, and you will be stunningly attractive.

Many of my coaching sessions lead to the client taking the affirmation, "I am enough." When you know you are enough, you bypass endless attempts to prove yourself and get the world to agree. You will save years or lifetimes of anxious effort. I live near a little town that gets congested with traffic in the afternoon. It can take a long time to get through the main street lined with shops and restaurants. A while back, the county constructed a bypass road for people who want to avoid the traffic. After just a few minutes on the bypass, you arrive on the other side of town. If you are busy clamoring to get all the stuff the world holds dear, including compliments and accolades, you will get stuck in the traffic where everyone is competing. If you are more interested in just living happily and authentically, you will bypass the madding crowd and cruise through your life without a lot of hassles.

The Question that Changes Everything

When I wrote my first book, *The Dragon Doesn't Live Here Anymore*, I was not trained as a writer and I knew nothing about the book industry. I simply wanted to express the ideas that inspired me, and hopefully uplift others. I didn't care if the book was famous or if I earned a lot of money. I felt as if I was birthing something meaningful, and I had to give it life. Unable to find a publisher, I published the book myself with borrowed money.

Through an amazing series of synchronicities, the book became a bestseller and I received unexpected income for it. My entire life changed and set me on the path that has led to the book you are now holding. While I was grateful for the response and income, those were not my goals. My goals were to deliver healing truth to the world. An English teacher told me, "The book is not technically perfect, but I felt your realness, which gave me the courage to live more authentically."

Years later a publisher requested me to write a testimonial for a book, *Sickened: The True Story of a Lost Childhood,* by Julie Gregory. The author's life as a child was hell because her mother projected all kinds of fake diseases onto her. The mother constantly took the girl to doctors and got them to prescribe all kinds of medications and treatments, for no good reason. The child narrowly escaped open heart surgery. Her crazy mother nearly drove her crazy.

When Julie grew up, she took a college psychology course in which the professor described the syndrome as "factitious disorder imposed on another." In a shocking flash, she realized that this was the story of her childhood. There was never anything wrong with her at all. Her self-image of being a sick person with many diseases was a huge lie. This realization set Julie off on a path of spiritual self-discovery.

As I read *Sickened*, I wondered why the publisher had sent it to me for an endorsement. Then I read a passage where Julie reported that she had found my book and took it to a remote cabin where she holed up, read it, and did intensive inner growth work that changed her life. Reading this, tears came to my eyes. How that book found its way to Julie was a miracle, orchestrated by a hand that went far beyond anything I could plan or control. The same source that gave me the book dispatched it to the people who could benefit from it. I felt deeply humbled to be part of that process.

The great Orchestrator will also deliver your gifts to the people who can most benefit from them. But you have to give the universe something to work with. You must turn your inspiration and ideas into tangible expression. If you produce in order to generate a return, your gifts will be diluted. If you produce to bless the world, your gifts will be empowered, and the return will exceed your expectations. You are not being egotistical in expressing yourself. It is ego that keeps you from expressing yourself. Humility assures you that you are being guided.

The most effective cure for stage fright is to shift from the self-absorbed question, "What will people think of me?"

to "How might this help others?" My spiritual guide Hilda was once a classical dancer who presented her unique creations at many famous venues. Hilda told me, "I used to get nervous before a performance. I was afraid I would fall onstage or that people would criticize my unusual dances. Then one night before my performance I looked from the stage wing out at the audience, and the thought came to me, 'Maybe I can enhance these people's lives with my dance. Maybe I can lighten the burdens they carry.' In that moment my fear disappeared and never returned. When I shifted from 'What can I get?' to 'How can I help?' I stepped into the real purpose and deeper reward of my career."

Humility, Not Humiliation

Humility does not mean that you say disparaging things about yourself, cast yourself as inferior to others, or spend your life apologizing. That's humiliation. I work with many Japanese people who come from a culture that has honed humility to a high and noble art. I have learned life-changing lessons from the extraordinary kindness of the Japanese people. We in the West could benefit immensely from incorporating such humility in our lives.

But some Japanese people take humility to an extreme, and drop into self-belittling. They feel they are unworthy of healthy, happy relationships, a passionate career, abundant income, or a life of joy, creativity, and self-expression. They have been taught that their happiness will somehow take away from the happiness of others. A lot of my work with Japanese clients is to help them realize that they deserve radiant well-being, and they do not need to sacrifice their joy to contribute to society—to the contrary, their joy *is* their contribution to society. When they receive this great realization, their lives change in wonderful ways.

True humility means that you know that God created you for a good reason, and your Creator wants you to bring your whole self to the world. Empty of ego, magnificent results accrue through you, and life rewards you spiritually and materially. Don't push away the blessings available to you and to others through you because you feel less-than. That's false humility. Real humility accepts the greatness of God as an attribute of yourself. Then you go about the business of uplifting the world as a co-creation between you and Higher Power.

Jesus Christ was one of the most powerful souls ever to walk the Earth, and one of the humblest. He allowed God to use his mind, personality, and body to extricate others from pain and guide them to well-being. He washed the feet of his disciples, demonstrating that no one is so important that he cannot take care of others and honor the God in them. Jesus said, "The last shall be first, and the first last." Those who seem least in the world's hierarchy of values will shine the brightest, and those at the top of the ladder of power will be stuck in a bog. *A Course in Miracles* tells us, "Be humble before God, but great in Him."

Jesus was born in a secluded cave, and after his crucifixion his body was laid in a cave. He entered the world in a humble space, and he achieved the resurrection in another place removed from the world. It's hard to hear the voice of God if you are distracted by the trinkets and trophies the world dangles before us. At some point we value inner peace more than building empires. All worldly empires are but dust in the face of the kingdom of love.

When John the Baptist met Jesus, he said, "I must decrease so he can increase." Ego evaporates in the presence of love. The light of Spirit is so bright that you want it to fill your whole world. You gladly surrender your need to control, and doubts are replaced with trust and gratitude. All emptiness is filled, and you are held firmly in the arms of God.

A Place to Lay
Your Head

When I ask my seminar audiences, "Who among you feels like you don't fit into the world?" most people raise their hand. I tell them, "You are in good company. Neither did Jesus Christ." He, too, felt like a stranger in a strange land.

> Foxes have dens and birds of the air have nests,
> but the Son of Man has no place to lay His head.

If you, too, feel like there is nowhere in the world you can find rest, that's because the world is not your home. As a spiritual being, you will not find peace in the material plane. Three or four dimensions are too small to contain an eternal soul.

Your real home is in heaven. Nothing less will bring you the happiness you crave and deserve.

If you have gone from relationship to relationship, job to job, teacher to teacher, or house to house, you might worry that there is something wrong with you. But actually there is something right with you. You will not find contentment in the world of opposites. You will find it only in your deep abiding wholeness.

Buddhists are called to take refuge in the Buddha. Likewise, we can take refuge in Christ. A refugee is someone who flees from his country because of war, political upheaval, social injustice, famine, or disease. He recognizes there is a safer and more secure place for him and his family to thrive. He leaves a place of turmoil and emigrates to a place of stability. Taking refuge in Christ or Buddha means to renounce your search to find safety in a land of war, and instead find comfort where peace is your birthright, and cannot be removed by people or conditions.

Life Beyond Medication

I also ask my audiences, "How do you medicate your pain?" I am referring not just to physical pain, but to fear, upset, and stress. Participants come up with some revealing answers: *Drinking. Smoking cigarettes or weed. Antidepressants and pain killers. Web surfing, texting, and social media. Watching television. Impersonal sex. Overworking. Compulsive shopping. Mindless talk and banter. Neurotically controlling my environment. Arguing over politics. Obsessive exercise. Sports fanaticism.* While there is nothing wrong with most of these activities in their essential pure form, many people use them to avoid dealing with their anxiety. They are numbing themselves rather than healing themselves.

It is right and natural to do whatever you can to get out of pain. *How* you release yourself determines whether you will get free or remain bound. Some people resign themselves to hardship and wait to die to be liberated; they believe that suffering is their ticket to paradise. Others carve escape routes through the methods I listed above. Such "medications" provide a temporary respite. But the next morning when you wake up with a hangover, or your lover leaves, or you get your credit card bill after a shopping spree, you are right back where you started, in deeper distress. Your escape attempt was just a band-aid. It soothed the symptom for a bit, but did not penetrate to the source of your stress. You tore the leaf off the weed, but did not pull up the root.

To truly get out of pain, we must go beyond masking symptoms, and take refuge in a higher truth. Letting Jesus or another spiritual master heal you means that you join him in the state of mind he or she attained. Think of inner peace as a room in your mind. This room is open to anyone who wishes to enter at any time. Jesus found his way to this room, and beckons you to join him. "And if I go and prepare a place for you, I will come back and welcome you into my presence, so that you also may be where I am."

Rest for Your Soul

A lot of us have gotten so used to life being hard that when it gets easy, or at least easier, we grow suspicious. *There must be some devil waiting in the wings. This is too good to be true. I don't know who I would be if I were not struggling.* Yet Christ wants our lives to be free of pain. He understands the suffering that most people undergo, and he offers a way out:

> Come to me, all of you who are weary and burdened, and I will give you rest. Take my yoke upon you and learn from me; for I am gentle and humble in heart, and you will find rest for your soul.

The glorification of suffering is the most tragic distortion of Christ's teachings. I have counseled countless people who are unable to relax or enjoy their lives because they believe that if they are not bearing some cross, they are failing God's requirement to squirm. If Jesus were to return today and tell it like he meant it, his first proclamation would be to get over the need to bleed.

God does not want you to suffer any more than you want your children to suffer. "If a man's son asked for a loaf of bread, would he give him a stone? And if he asked for a fish, would he give him a serpent?" Jesus presented many teachings that call us to be kind to ourselves and take good care of our body and soul. Yet these parables have gotten buried under convoluted misinterpretations and burdensome edicts. Let us now take the gleaming sword of St. Michael and slice away teachings that lead us to pain instead of peace.

Let God Do the Heavy Lifting

A yoke is the wooden crosspiece fastened across the necks of two animals joined together to pull a plow. "Take my yoke upon you" means, "Partner with me. I will do the heavy pulling and your part will be easy." "Learn from me" means, "Use me as a role model of allowing Spirit to work through you. When you quit trying to do it all yourself and you let God pull the plow, your soul will come to rest."

I often quote the following passage from *A Course in Miracles* because its life-changing vision cannot be overstated.

> When you have learned how to decide with God, all decisions become as easy and as right as breathing. There is no effort, and you will be led as gently as if you were being carried down a quiet path in summer.

This lovely image certainly sounds a lot more attractive than bearing the old rugged cross, wouldn't you agree? You are free to make a case for the value of suffering if you wish, but you will inherit the results of your argument. As Richard Bach stated in his brilliant book *Illusions*, "Argue for your limitations, and, sure enough, they are yours." Make a stand for ease, on the other hand, and you will enjoy blessings that self-beating will never incur.

All crucifixion is self-crucifixion. It may appear that other people or external forces are causing you pain, but you participate in what disturbs you. If you withdraw any value you ascribe to suffering, you will become free of it. We can simplify Jesus's yoke metaphor: "Life can be easier if you just let me help you."

Finding the Sweet Spot

We are well familiar with Jesus's call to "Consider the lilies of the field. They do not labor or spin their clothing. I tell you that Solomon in all his glory was not arrayed like one of these." But how many of us take his metaphor literally, and put his vision into action by refusing to worry?

Jesus is not asking us to quit our jobs and lay in the field with the lilies—although a stint of that might do us all some good. He is more specifically directing us to drop an *attitude* of struggle. Struggle seems to be a behavior, but it is really a mentality. Two people could be assigned the same task, and one of them sweats through it, while another dances through it. The woman who organizes my programs in Japan made a cute English spelling error in an email. "Let's find the sweat spot for how to present this program," she wrote. I giggled and told her that the proper spelling was "sweet spot." I suggested that we might title a seminar, "From the Sweat Spot to the Sweet Spot."

Jesus's lilies image brings us one more gift: You cannot improve on God's creation. When I stroll through a forest, sit beside a stream, or study a piece of driftwood on the beach, I marvel at the perfection before me. Every tree in the grove, rock in the stream, or smooth curve in the driftwood is an artistic masterpiece by the Creator. Even the dead leaves on the forest floor, or the knots on the driftwood are elements of their majesty. Then I consider the buildings we have erected, the airplanes we fly, and the medications we take. While all of these manufactured items have their place and purpose, they do not touch the quiet majesty of a redwood tree, the grandeur of an eagle in flight, or the restorative power of herbs without side effects. The more we try to improve on nature, the more we distance ourselves from it. Christ begs us to recognize the splendor given to us rather than attempting to override it. Then we will walk side by side with Christ in a world adorned with fragrant lilies rather than cloth ones.

The End of Earning

My friend Kyle is a dog trainer who is often stressed about his income. One day when I was visiting Kyle, I brought some treats for his house dogs. As I reached into my pocket for a cookie, one cute little pooch approached me and sat up, eagerly awaiting it. Kyle interrupted me, "Please wait. The dog has to work for it."

While I understand the importance of training, my friend's request gave me a clue as to why he is so frazzled. He does not believe he deserves any treats without working for them. What a burdensome mentality! It's time we revisit our belief that we must earn a living. In a culture driven by the work ethic, to suggest that you deserve to be taken care of by the universe is tantamount to heresy. Yet Jesus was the most heretical figure in history. His entire ministry was about overturning oppressive rules, mindless rituals, unfounded obligations, the belief in sin, and the need for punishment. The mystical messiah was, above all else, a liberator.

Jesus wants us to gauge our worth not by what we do, but by what we are. If you evaluate yourself on how well you perform, you will never become worthy. To the mind steeped in performance, there is always a higher notch we must reach for. While there is value in honest labor and striving to improve, the ego has twisted that process into a never-ending struggle to complete all the items on our to-do list today. People who evaluate themselves only on performance are occasionally satisfied, but often frustrated. While developing performance skills is a component of success in the world, the rules of the kingdom of heaven are entirely different than the rules of the world. They are, in fact, the direct opposite. While the world evaluates us on doing, heaven rewards us for being. While the world is motivated by filling in gaps, heaven acknowledges wholeness. While the world requires us to do tricks to earn our treats, heaven affirms that you deserve all the treats you want because you are a child of God, and everything in the kingdom belongs to you.

You can endure just so much struggle before you say, "I can't believe this is how I was born to live." That moment of stunning realization is the beginning of healing. The Son of Man—your true self—*does* have a place to lay his head. But it is not the one the world has shown you. It is the one your soul remembers. Your discomfort with life on Earth is not an unsolvable predicament. It is a call to look deeper. You are being guided to trade mystery for mastery; victim for victor; pushing against for allowing; doing for being. Quit trying to do God's job—that position is already filled. "When you work, God rests. When you rest, God works."

When we cease trying to fit into the world, we gain the power to master the world. You will be in smaller company, but company worth keeping. Better to fly with a few eagles than many crows. Your place in the cosmos does not require the agreement of the masses. It is but your own heart's approval that you need. Guided by Spirit, you may still walk through the motions of your daily activities, but your step is lighter, your breathing deeper. You *do* have a place in life, tailored by the universe just for you. That sacred space yields the comfort for your soul that you have not found in searching elsewhere. The time for the great homecoming is at hand.

WHO ENDS UP
AT THE BANQUET

While I was traveling through Chicago's O'Hare Airport, a storm blew in and my connecting flight was delayed. So I made my way to the crowded frequent flyer lounge for a few hours. As I took my seat, I heard a woman near me conducting a loud conversation on her cell phone. She was a stressed executive, rudely barking orders to her subordinates. She was not a happy camper.

Then the cleaning lady came by, picking up cups and trash from the tables. This woman beamed a lovely smile, asking if there was any way she could help the disgruntled patrons. She moved as gracefully as an angel, quietly lighting up the room,

201

offering a kind word to those she passed. I marveled at the contrast between the miserable high-powered executive and the radiant low-paid cleaning lady.

One of the most prevalent illusions is that people who are important in the world enjoy a more heavenly existence than common folks. Jesus reversed this myth in this parable:

A wealthy man planned a splendid banquet and invited many people. When the feast was ready, he sent his servant to tell all the invitees, "Come, for all is now ready." But they all made excuses. "I purchased a piece of land, and I must go see it." "I just bought five yokes of oxen, and I am going to check on them." "I recently got married, so I cannot attend."

The servant returned and reported that the guests had declined the invitations. The master grew angry and said to his servant, "Now go out into the streets and byways of the town and bring in the poor, the crippled, the blind, and the lame."

When the servant fulfilled the command, he said, "What you ordered has been done, and there is still room."

Then the master said to the servant, "Go out into the roads and lanes, and urge people to come in, so that my house may be filled. For I tell you, none of those who were invited will taste my dinner."

In Jesus's parables, the master or wealthy person represents God, and a banquet symbolizes the kingdom of heaven. In this story, God offers the kingdom of heaven to everyone, but the important people were too involved with their affairs to sit down at the feast. Not much has changed since Jesus painted that scenario. People are busier today than ever. If Jesus were here now, he might say, "Would you please just put down your phone long enough to take my call?"

The touching element of the parable is that there *was* a population who accepted the master's invitation—the poor, the crippled, the blind, and the lame. These people were available for two reasons: First, they had nothing better to do, since they were not preoccupied with managing their empires. Even more important, the troubles they had known had humbled them and made them receptive to help from a higher source. After weathering their hardships, they were highly motivated to receive a kingdom beyond the one that had marginalized them.

While you might identify with either the busy people or those in need, we all contain both elements in our psyche. Even if you are not wealthy or a celebrity, a part of you is engaged in worldly dramas that distract you from peace. And even if you are not poor, crippled, blind, or lame, some part of you is hurting and yearns for release from pain. This part of your mind is more likely to sit down to the banquet than the part that is preoccupied.

After Jesus delivered the parable, he uttered his famous statement, "Many are called but few are chosen." We might also say, "Many (actually all) are called, but few choose to heed the call." God does not pick a select few and cast the rest aside. We select or reject ourselves by the consciousness we hold. If you are open to receive blessings, they come and uplift you. If you are not open, or distracted, you miss them. God does not play favorites. We either favor ourselves or we don't.

The Choice Behind All Other Choices

I saw a sign on an executive's desk, "Anyone who is too busy to pray is too busy." We might likewise say that anyone who is too busy to step back and enjoy a moment of peace is too busy. You might pray, meditate, journal, do yoga or tai chi, paint, dance, play music, or walk in the woods. Any activity that connects you with your spiritual Source is a prayer. There are plenty of ways to receive the presence of love. No matter what form your connection time takes, it helps sustain you throughout your day so you don't get lost in worldly activities. I find it extremely helpful to start my day with meditation, and then clear my mind before I go to sleep. Brief check-ins during the day also maintain your seat at the banquet.

The key to accepting the Great Invitation is to recognize that the banquet that heaven offers is far more satisfying than any the world provides. The ego interprets prayer or meditation time as a sacrifice. "Let's just get this over with so I can get back to my work and errands." But there is no sacrifice in healing or claiming the kingdom of love. You are giving up a little in exchange for a lot.

If the invitees in the parable realized what a gift they were being offered, they would have gladly dropped their worldly activities and rushed to sit down at the feast of heaven. What could be more attractive or rewarding than deep inner peace and total happiness? That is the choice before us each day.

Closing the Gap

Another way we miss the banquet is to set up prerequisites for happiness. We believe that inner peace is available in the future, but not now. If you wait until you lose ten pounds, get your degree, or remodel your house, fulfillment will always be around the next corner. Most of us live in a nebulous gap between where we are and where we want to be.

But there is no such gap. If there seems to be one, it is because you have made up a story that something is missing. But nothing is missing. The key phrase in the parable is, "Come, for all is now ready." Not in ten minutes, ten months, or ten years. *Now.* If you can claim well-being now, it will also be available when then becomes now. If you miss joy now, the next "then" will not be different than your current experience.

I know a woman who participated in an intensive week-end personal growth program. During the seminar, Donna confronted her fears and discovered the beauty, power, and worth within her. "When I left that program, my eyes were opened, and the entire world was filled with majesty and delight," she explained. "Nothing outside me had changed. My vision had simply clarified. What once looked like hell suddenly became heaven."

This is the transformation of consciousness that Jesus came to deliver to humanity. He spoke constantly of the kingdom of heaven because he wanted to take us there with him. Religions have placed far too much emphasis on avoiding hell, and far too little on claiming heaven. Jesus wanted to keep our minds focused on the highest reward. You don't escape from hell by magnifying it or fearfully running from it. Fear *is* hell, so if you fear hell, you are already there. You escape from hell by accepting heaven instead.

Even while a part of your mind is distracted, another part—the realest part—is established in wholeness. Jesus said, "Neither will they say, 'Look, here!' or, 'Look, there!' for behold, the kingdom of God is within you." The spiritual journey is not about traveling anywhere. It is about recognizing that what you seek, you already are. It is about claiming the heaven you already own. God has given all, but we experience only what we are willing to receive.

Businesspeople make offers with deadlines. If you are purchasing a home, for example, you present an offer that is good until a certain day and time. There is a window of opportunity for the seller to accept your offer. The window of opportunity to accept the kingdom of heaven is always open. No matter how many times you have turned down the invitation, or been distracted elsewhere, the God of mercy and grace is happy to welcome you. The banquet is laid out. Shall we sit and dine?

RESISTANCE
IS FUTILE

In a *Star Trek* television series, the crew of the Starship Enter-prise engages in ongoing battle with the Borg, a nasty race of biochemical parasites determined to engulf and destroy all beings they encounter. The Borg continuously tell the Enterprise's crew, "Resistance is futile."

On another sound stage galaxies and centuries away, Jesus Christ told his followers, "Resist not evil, but overcome evil with good." How interesting that evil tells good that resistance is futile, and good tells evil the same! Yet "the devil quotes scrip-ture," and ego twists truth for its own purposes.

In advising us not to resist evil, Jesus delivered an advanced metaphysical lesson that we have touched on before, and will now explore in depth: We empower what we fight. What we give our attention to, grows in our experience. The key to get rid of evil is to quit feeding it by focusing on it, especially with strong emotions. When you infuse your thoughts with intense feelings, you energize them. When you get upset, angry, or outraged by any person, organization, or act, you give it immense power. Then you attract more of that experience. The biblical character Job said, "What I feared has come upon me." Not because God hurls suffering at us, but because we manifest what we think and feel.

Jesus delivered the nonresistance principle in many different ways:

If a man strikes you on one cheek, offer him the other.

If a man in authority asks you to walk
a mile with him, walk with him two.

If someone takes your coat, give him your cloak as well.

Give to everyone who asks you, and if anyone
takes what is yours, do not demand it back.

Agree with your adversary quickly.

Pray for those who persecute you.

A Course in Miracles reiterates the same teaching in modern language:

> Recognize what does not matter, and if your
> brothers ask you for something "outrageous,"
> do it because it does not matter.

When you fight over money, a material object, real estate, an inheritance, who washes the dishes, who controls the TV remote, what color to paint the living room, or whether the toilet tissue should roll from the wall or the other side, you are attributing undue importance to something that is unimportant. The world is a blank screen upon which we project our beliefs. Things have only the meaning we give them with our mind. When you argue over something, you give it power over your happiness. You might criticize someone for being stuck on a particular outcome, but if you demand the opposite outcome, you are stuck too. You are both spinning on the same karmic wheel of attributed meaning. Such conflicts end only when one person withdraws his or her insistence to have his or her way. *A Course in Miracles* asks, "Would you prefer to be right, or happy?" You may win a battle, but it is only a matter of time until the next skirmish eclipses your peace. Life is not about winning wars. It is about ending them.

Heated religionists don't realize that when they fight evil, they are making more evil. The goal is noble, but the method is flawed. Eastern religions like Buddhism, Taoism, and Shintoism also seek to create well-being on Earth, but they do not fight the world. Instead, they rise above it. The fear-based mind seeks (like the Borg) to attack and destroy everything by which it feels threatened. So we marshal wars on poverty, drugs, drunk drivers, teenage pregnancy, and an endless list of diseases, with very few positive results. The secret to ending these troubles is not to wrestle with the unwanted behavior, but to rise to a higher perspective. We end poverty by modeling prosperity. We ameliorate teenage pregnancy by inspiring teens about the value of relationship and edifying their self-worth. We overcome disease by recognizing that disease operates at one frequency while health operates at another; when we uplevel our vibration, disease cannot touch us. All of these transformational tools do not include any form of warfare. They are all based on removing attention from the object of resistance, and focusing on the desired experience instead.

The methods I just suggested are interpersonal. Yet the deeper key to transforming the outer world is to heal our own mind. If you are disturbed by poverty, you must erase a belief in lack from your mindset. Before seeking to rid the roads of drunk drivers, consider if you hold any out-of-control thoughts that pose a danger to yourself or those in your field of influence. If you wish to eradicate global disease, ask yourself, "Am I living any lifestyle patterns that diss (or deny) ease?" Internal growth organically spills to bless everyone you touch. When you end the troubles in your own psyche, you are in the perfect position to become an effective world change agent.

Why Complaining Doesn't Work

Any form of complaining distances us from peace. Griping is a negative vortex that sucks the complainer in like quicksand. Complaining fixates on what is not working at the expense of what is working or could work. There is value, of course, in identifying a situation that needs to be improved and then taking action to better it. The key is to hold the vision of the completed project even while you are moving toward it. I heard a Christian minister confess, "I am a hypocrite. I say I believe in Jesus Christ and his teaching of our innate perfection, and then I grumble about my pains." As godly beings, we were born to live fully blessed. All else is a delusion, a distraction, a compromise. When we complain, we deny the kingdom and momentarily remove ourselves from it.

Just as we have chosen to step away from heaven, we can choose to re-enter it. The gates of grace are always open. You are never more than one thought away from peace. Many people have experienced a miraculous physical, emotional, or spiritual healing in an instant. The Apostle Paul said, "Change can come in a flash, the twinkling of an eye."

Believing that peace awaits at the end of a long, hard road is a subtle form of resistance. In waiting for your good, you miss the good before you now. You can set up your life so you achieve healing after a great deal of struggle and effort, but that is a self-fulfilling prophecy. You can also achieve healing the moment you are open and willing to receive it. Behold the opportunity our loving Source has bestowed upon us.

Where to Turn Your Cheek

"Turn the other cheek" does not mean that we should allow people to keep hurting us. If you are in an abusive relationship, job, or living situation, you must extricate yourself, either by upgrading the situation or leaving. There is no spiritual value in putting up with pain; martyrdom is an old model we have outgrown. Your happiness is your gift to the universe. When you remove yourself from a toxic situation, you help the person who is mistreating you, as well as yourself. People who engage in abusive behaviors dig themselves into a deeper hole, making more negative karma they will have to undo. When you leave a toxic situation, you support the other person to break free of an unhealthy pattern. Your departure can be a wake-up call for them, if they are willing to receive it. You are affirming, "I deserve better, and so do you."

Turning the other cheek means to look in another direction, to see more clearly from a different perspective. The new direction might be, "I can enjoy a happy, healthy relationship," or "now I know what I don't want, so I can claim what I do want," or "this is my opportunity to break a longtime pattern and become a master rather than a victim." Or, simply, "I could see peace instead of this." When we use a painful situation to think less with fear and more with love, the experience serves us well. Then we graduate from an important lesson, and move forward, empowered.

Growing Beyond Evil

We can reframe acts and situations that appear to be evil by seeing them through the lens of compassion. For example, Matthew 7:11 is translated in almost all Bible versions, "If you, then, who are evil, know how to give good gifts to your children, how much more will your Father in heaven give good gifts to those who ask Him!" Yet the Weymouth New Testament translates, "If you then, *imperfect as you are*, know how to give good gifts to your children, how much more will your Father in heaven give good things to those who ask Him!"

Personally, I would rather be imperfect than evil, and I imagine so would you. (We are all inherently perfect, but the jump from evil to perfection may be more than some of us can handle. But from evil to imperfect feels doable.) Here we can see how much judgment and guilt is infused in many Bible translations. That golden volume should yield us greater freedom, not more oppression. If you knew that all you would ever receive from God is love, compassion, kindness, forgiveness, and grace, would you not eagerly fall into the arms of your divine parent? This is the God that Jesus Christ came to introduce to the world. When you know *that* God and you take refuge in Him/Her, Christ's mission is fulfilled, along with yours.

The Destiny of Visionary Thought

It turns out that the Borg were correct; resistance *is* futile. Fighting anything is a self-defeating campaign because we are already greater than the object we battle. Yet the Borg were essentially impotent because their fear-based vendetta had no foundation in truth. What is not of love eventually cancels itself out. When you fight something, you stoop to its frequency rather than holding a higher one. Instead, make a stand for what you believe in without energizing what you detest.

Monumental social change agents like Lincoln, Gandhi, and King succeeded because they kept their eye on the goal rather than obstacles to it. They did not cast their opponents as evil; they simply stood for the freedom they wanted to replace oppression. (Abraham Lincoln said, "I don't like that man. I must get to know him.") You can walk the same high road by releasing a need to battle, and knowing that you deserve your heart's desires. When Jesus said, "Ask and it is given," the asking he was referring to was not in words. It is establishing your consciousness in where you want to arrive, not what you are turning away from. Visionary thought always lands at its chosen destination. The universe would have it no other way.

THE GOD
OF ONLY LOVE

While Jesus was at a dinner in his honor, a woman of
poor reputation barged into the gathering. She knelt
before the master and began to weep, her tears falling on Jesus's
feet. She wiped them with her hair, and then brought forth a
vial of expensive perfume and anointed Jesus's feet.

Religious onlookers, outraged that such a woman had pene-
trated their assembly and touched Jesus as she did, demanded
that she be removed. The master told them, "Do not stop her."
He lifted the woman's chin, looked into her eyes, and told her,
"Your sins—and I know they are many—are forgiven. Your faith
has saved you."

The Pharisees were still fuming. "You cannot forgive this
woman!" they cried out. "Only God can forgive sins."

Jesus responded by telling them this parable:

A certain lender had two debtors. One owed him five hundred denarii, and the other, fifty. When they couldn't pay, he forgave them both. Which of them will therefore love the lender most?

The disciple Simon, sitting beside Jesus, answered, "The one whom he forgave the most."

Jesus replied, "You are correct . . . He who is little forgiven loves the least."

Likewise, he or she who is greatly forgiven, loves the most. When the Pharisees criticized Jesus for spending so much time with sinners, he answered,

Which of you, if you had one hundred sheep, and lost one of them, wouldn't leave the ninety-nine, and go after the one that was lost, until he found it? When he has found it, he carries it on his shoulders, rejoicing. When he comes home, he calls together his friends, family, and neighbors, and tells them, "Celebrate with me, for I have found my lost sheep!" Likewise, there will be more joy in heaven over one sinner who is redeemed, than over ninety-nine righteous people who need no redemption."

Let us replace the word "sinner" with "those who believe they have sinned and are beyond the love of God." Or, "those who are in extreme physical or emotional pain." We can rephrase the lesson of the parable: "If someone is in great pain, do they not deserve more attention than others who are in little or no pain?"

When the Pharisees argued, "No man has the power to grant forgiveness," they were in part correct. No person can give forgive because in God's eyes we are already forgiven. A person who forgives is simply affirming a condition that already exists. *A Course in Miracles* tells us, "God does not forgive because He never has condemned." Even God cannot grant forgiveness because in the mind of God there was never anything to forgive. Forgiveness is not a change in condition, but a change in awareness. In the mind of God, the only condition is love. No other experience can intrude on heaven. Our role is not to reverse the verdict of punishment, but to recognize that God never issued such a verdict. *A Course in Miracles* tells us that whenever we stand before God's court, the only verdict is "case dismissed."

The Dissolution of a Wrathful God

I meet many people who have turned their back on religion, spirituality, or God. They were raised in a religion or family that terrified them with stories of a vicious, bloodthirsty deity. They were taught that they were evil sinners, and if they did not live a perfectly saintly life, they would burn in hell for eternity. I don't blame these people for hating such a religion. Who would want to live suffocated with threat and punishment? Surely there must be a better way.

Jesus Christ delivered that way of mercy and compassion. Although fearful people have projected their murky beliefs onto Christ and inserted harsh words in his mouth, his ministry and message were devoted to freeing human beings from the oppression of a wrathful God.

If you knew that God is love and only love, how would you be living differently? If you could erase fear and guilt from your mind and heart, what would you do, and what would you stop doing? If you recognized yourself as innocent, perfect just as you are, who would you see when you look in the mirror?

Jesus came to replace original sin with original innocence. He removed an angry, fire-breathing God from the throne of terror, and instituted a God of only love. We must question, challenge, and grow beyond any notion that God is anything but love. This realization changes everything!

Live Like You're Loved

One of the ways to activate a new life is to live as if it's already so. Some people say, "fake it 'til you make it." But that's a misnomer. The suggestion assumes that you are a loser faking you are a winner until you become a winner. This idea is upside down. You are a winner acting like a winner until you know that you are a winner. A more appropriate advice would be, "faith it 'til you make it."

One of my favorite songs is, "Live Like You're Loved" by Hawk Nelson. This is the meditation of a lifetime! Take a moment now to consider if you are living like you are loved, or if instead you are living like you are deprived, guilty, or condemned. If you are accepting any form of lack, judgment, abuse, or illness, you have overlooked your birthright of abundance, freedom, kindness, and vibrant health. None of those negative conditions come from God. They proceed from erroneous thoughts we have unknowingly accepted.

I have coached thousands of people who suffer from a sense of unworthiness. In every case, we can trace the person's harsh self-criticism back to a parent, sibling, relative, teacher, authority figure, or religion that laid judgments over the child. No child is born with a poor self-image. Guilt is entirely learned. The judgments that bind us are not our own. They were adopted from people who did not love themselves and attempted to relieve their pain by projecting it onto us. When we replace dark beliefs with the love we once knew but have forgotten, transformation follows. Healing is not a new state that we achieve. It is a glorious homecoming.

It's Not Your Fault

I saw a documentary about the Burning Man festival, a huge gathering that takes place every year in the Nevada desert. As many as eighty thousand people come together for a celebration of creativity, art, and uplifting community.

In this film, a fellow went around to people and told them, "It's not your fault." He had never met these individuals and he knew nothing about them. He simply told them, "It's not your fault." The reactions of the recipients were astounding. Some people broke into tears. Others' faces lit up with huge relief. Others laughed joyfully. We all labor under the belief that something is our fault, and we beat ourselves for our assumed transgression. When this man told those people, "It's not your fault," they were released from their self-imposed burden.

We can sum up Jesus Christ's entire ministry as, "It's not your fault." When he forgave the adulterous woman and the sinful woman who anointed his feet, he was saying, "It's not your fault." When he dined with hated tax collectors and he healed the servant of the Roman centurion, whose army was oppressing Israel, he was demonstrating, "It's not your fault." When he uttered from the cross, "Forgive them, Father, for they know not what they do," he was declaring, "It's not your fault."

Nothing would make Jesus Christ happier than for us to agree with him, "It's not my fault." Take a moment now and think of something you feel guilty, embarrassed, or ashamed about. Then imagine that the fellow at Burning Man, or someone you love, or Jesus himself, takes your hands, looks deeply into your eyes, and tells you, "It's not your fault." If you can receive this forgiveness, you finally know yourself as God knows you.

Burning Man drew its name from the climax event of the festival, the dramatic burning of a huge wooden effigy of a person. The climax of our journey into the dark world of fear is the undoing of the broken or evil person you thought you were. An old, tired, wretched identity is going up in flames, brilliant against the backdrop of the desert night. In the aftermath of the undoing stands a Christlike figure, the phoenix rising from the ashes. The god of guilt has been supplanted by the God of only love, and we are free.

GOD WALKS THE
WORLD AS YOU

Sandi had not spoken to her sister Claudia in ten years. Then one day she received a phone call from Claudia, from an unknown telephone number. "Where are you calling from?" Sandi asked.

"A while back I bought a house in St. Helena," Claudia replied. "A few years ago a fire raged through the area, and every house was destroyed except mine. Today I was looking at a small plaque on my living room wall. It shows a Japanese symbol. I turned to the back of the plaque and found a description. The symbol means, 'water.' The explanation said, 'If you keep this plaque in your house, you will be protected from fire.'"

Sandi was stunned. Her sister calling her was uncharacteristic. Beyond that, Claudia's house was miraculously spared.

"Then I remembered something," Claudia went on. "Thirty years ago, you gave me that plaque."

When you perform an act of kindness, you never know how far its ripples will extend. *A Course in Miracles* tells us, "A miracle is never lost. It may touch many people you have not even met, and produce undreamed of changes in situations of which you are not even aware." When Sandi gave Claudia that plaque, she had no idea that the gift would eventually bless her sister in a miraculous way.

Why God Needs You

God works through people. Jesus Christ did not descend from a cloud and hose down Claudia's house so the fire would not consume it. Instead, the Christ mind inspired Sandi to offer an act of kindness that would one day help her sister enormously and contribute to their reconciliation.

Christ is equally ready and able to work through you. Food does not usually magically appear before a hungry person, and a house does not sprout from the ground to shelter a family in need. But caring people serve meals at homeless shelters, and organizations like Habitat for Humanity build homes as gifts. Such acts are just as much miracles as if the meal or house manifested out of nowhere. We deliver blessings in co-creation with Higher Power. In *A Course in Miracles,* Jesus also tells us, "You are my voice, my eyes, my feet, my hands through which I save the world." While many people are waiting for Jesus Christ to redeem the world, God has already bestowed us with that momentous assignment. We are the channels through which divinity makes the world more like heaven.

Don't Heed the Doubt Voice

The chief impediment against people working miracles is self-doubt. *Who am I to deliver great things to the world? If you knew my secret sins, you would not love me or want me. I must get my own act together before I can add value to other people's lives.* It is not so. Great people struggle with many of the same issues that you and I do. The difference between world change agents and most people is that the change agents move forward with their flaws and foibles.

Even Moses suffered from a sense of unworthiness. When God called him to free the Hebrew nation from bondage in Egypt, Moses resisted, arguing that he had a speech impediment. One of the most influential spokesmen of all time was "heavy of mouth and heavy of tongue." That did not stop God from working through Moses. Likewise, your perceived deficiencies will not stop God from working through you. Don't use your humanity as an excuse to deny your divinity.

Great Spirit delivers healing by planting seeds of intuition, inspiration, and passion in our heart. Your inner voice is the voice of God speaking to you directly. Don't allow your hypercritical intellect to override your inner guidance. Give God a chance to bless the world through you.

Divinity Cloaked as Humanity

The popular song, "From a Distance" portrayed God as watching us. Lovely as the lyrics and music are, the song denies the presence of God in and among us. The idea of God stationed somewhere in outer space, observing and judging us, reinforces the illusion that God is a kind of Santa Claus sitting at the

North Pole watching humanity on a webcam, keeping score on who is naughty and who is nice. More accurate lyrics would be, "God is living us." God is just as much on this side of the clouds as beyond them. He/She/It is not interested in judging us, and more interested in helping us peel away the illusion that there is a gap between us and our Source.

Every person you meet is Christ asking, "Do you recognize me?" Are you seeing a broken body, or a vital spirit? Are you put off by crazy personalities, or do you remember the loveliness of a soul? To thrive in the world, we must use a kind of x-ray vision, piercing beyond the world people created into the world as God knows it. All that lives bears witness to holiness. Mystics stand in awe of the tiniest blade of dew-laden grass, a fluttering hummingbird, and an elephant trumpeting. Despite our foolish actions, human beings are the crowning glory of God's creation. Wherever life is, God is. Wherever we are, God is.

Christ might even show up as the person you see when you look in the mirror. While you may be fixated on your wrinkles, double chin, or thin lips, the Son of God is shining through your eyes and beaming through your smile. He is waiting for you to see yourself through his eyes.

The spirit of Christ refuses to be contained in one person or relegated to someone outside yourself. He needs people like you to move fearlessly into the heart of humanity and transform it from within it. He is looking for volunteers to do for the world what you think he should do for the world.

You Give Life Purpose

The world would have no purpose without you being here. Without humanity, beauty would have no one to enjoy it. God created the world in order to experience it uniquely through each of us. If you were a parent and you bought your kids a colorful playground set, you would set it up in your back yard for your children to enjoy. If they never saw it and no one played on it, it would be purposeless. The toy has meaning and value only when someone puts it to good use.

We are the children of God on the playground of Earth. Everything is set up for our appreciation and our education. All experiences are either to be enjoyed or learned from. The fun moments remind us how good it can get, and the hard moments deliver us lessons about how to live better. Either way, we win.

Many Christians quote the Bible verse, "For God so loved the world that He gave His only begotten Son . . ." The idea is that God sacrificed Jesus Christ so that we may all have life. *A Course in Miracles* makes the slightest edit in this language that makes a world of difference in its interpretation: "God so loved the world that He gave it *to* His only begotten son." Heaven is not purchased with sacrifice, but received as a gift of love. Jesus himself twice quoted Hosea 6:6: "I delight in mercy, not sacrifice." If God finds no value in sacrifice, why would he sacrifice His Son?

Jesus Christ was not an only child. We are all equally offspring of God. The original Greek language version of the Bible reads "Jesus Christ is Son of God." In that language there was no article as an element of grammar. Interpreters translated "the Son of God" when the meaning was "a son of God," implying that there are other sons or daughters of God—all of us. Jesus did not have any more God in him than we do. He was simply fully aware of the God in him, and he calls us to join him in that divine recognition.

You were born to bring a particular expression of Godness to the world. Your special emanation is as unique as your fingerprint or a snowflake. We love to be around babies and little children because they remember who they are, and have not yet been taught soul-depleting beliefs in comparison and competition. President Theodore Roosevelt said, "Comparison is the thief of joy." You can deliver all of your unique gifts and talents without infringing on anyone else's; the sum total of human expression makes the mosaic complete.

God's Gift to You

To believe that the world was created as a gift to you is not an expression of ego. To the contrary, to refute that you are beloved of your heavenly parent is a statement of vast denial. *A Course in Miracles* offers this poetic description of your unspeakable worth:

> All things that live bring gifts to you, and offer them in gratitude and gladness at your feet. The scent of flowers is their gift to you. The waves bow down before you, and the trees extend their arms to shield you from the heat, and lay their leaves before you on the ground that you may walk in softness, while the wind sinks to a whisper round your holy head.

The purpose of your spiritual path, and all of your life, is to remember and reclaim your identity as a divine being. All events and experiences are in the service of that superb awakening. Count nothing as outside that noble vision. When you finally realize that God walks the world as you, the big picture of your life will come into focus, and your entire journey will make perfect sense.

32

YOUR DIVINE
AUTHORITY

At some point in our life, each of us must make a crucial choice: Does the world have power over you, or do you determine your experience? Are you the slave of conditions, or do you command conditions with your consciousness? Are you the effect of external causes, or does life play out your intentions?

> When he got into the boat, his disciples followed him. Then there arose a great storm on the sea, so that the boat was being covered with the waves; but Jesus was asleep. And they came to him and woke him, saying, "Save us, Lord; we are perishing!"

He said to them, "Why are you afraid, you of little faith?" Then he got up and rebuked the winds and the sea, and they became perfectly calm. The men were amazed, and said, "What kind of a man is this, that even the winds and the sea obey him?"

Like the disciples aboard the boat, you might feel that the troubles of the world loom so threatening that you are in mortal danger and your ship is about to sink. Yet even while the angry swells approach, there is one sleeping in the hull, a healer established in your subconscious mind. This internal master has the power to quell the wind and waves.

There is an even more subtle teaching in this story: Jesus was sleeping so soundly that he was not even aware of the outer chaos. Turbulence was not in his reality. The ship was rocking, but not his mind. Likewise, your true self is established in peace independent of worldly conditions. Only the small self that gives its power away to outer circumstances can be upset.

Jesus, master of compassion, stepped up from the subconscious, met the disciples on the deck of worldly observation, and spoke the word that calmed the outer chaos. When faced with any form of tribulation, if you call upon the Christ within you, you gain dominion over even the harshest of circumstances.

The incident of Jesus walking on water, also recounted in the gospels, teaches the same lesson. Metaphysically, water represents emotions. Walking on water symbolizes rising above base feelings, thinking clearly, and getting to your destination without being distracted or overcome by emotional upset. The Christ within you cannot sink.

Take Back the Gifts That Were Stolen

People who have issues with authority figures don't realize that the authority within them is infinitely more powerful than any person who shows up on the movie screen of their life. When the Soviet Union was under Communist rule, I went with a group of citizen diplomats to build bridges of trust and love between our country and the Soviet people. There we made many friends and established deep heart connections.

The last evening of our visit, we had a farewell banquet. One member of our group invited a newfound Russian friend to join us, and we gave him some gifts. Meanwhile, several KGB secret police goons had infiltrated our gathering to spy on us. When they saw the young Russian man holding the gifts we had given him, one officer began to take the gifts from him. Seeing this, our group member Tom Sewell intervened. He boldly lifted the gifts one by one from the KGB man's hands, and replaced them in the arms of the citizen. Tom's intention was so strong that the KGB guy just stood there and watched the interaction. Then he shrank away, leaving the fellow with the gifts he rightfully deserved.

This inspiring scenario is a modern parable. You have been given magnificent gifts by a loving God who wishes to be your friend and support you. Meanwhile a creepy voice in your mind says, "You don't deserve this. I will take your happiness away from you." Then a savior in your mind reminds you, "You *do* deserve this. I will restore to you what is rightfully yours." The authority with which your inner savior speaks and acts is compelling and unopposable. The voice of fear is no match for the voice of love. It must yield, and leave you in God's beneficent care.

Christ Validates You

Jesus doesn't just want you to know how close to God he is. He wants you to know how close to God you are.

Winston Churchill's mother Jenny Jerome attended a dinner party where she met two politicians vying for the office of Prime Minister of the United Kingdom. Benjamin Disraeli and William Gladstone, she found, displayed sharply different personalities. During her conversation with Gladstone, he spent most of the time voicing his political opinions. Disraeli, on the other hand, took a sincere interest in Ms. Jerome and asked her many questions about her life and ideas. After the party, a journalist inquired about her impression of the two men. "When I left the dining room after sitting next to Gladstone, I thought he was the cleverest man in England," she replied. "But when I sat next to Disraeli, I left feeling that I was the cleverest woman." Disraeli went on to win the election and serve as one of England's most memorable leaders.

Those who heard Jesus's words from his own lips also felt uplifted and affirmed:

> When Jesus finished saying these things, the crowds were astonished at His teaching, because He taught as one who had real authority, quite unlike the teachers of religious law.

When the Bible tells us that Jesus spoke with authority, there were two elements to the power of his communication. The first is that he impressed people with his stunning connection to Source. The second is that he impressed people with *their* stunning connection to Source. Any teacher who says or implies, "I have the answer and you don't" is a half-teacher. Whole teachers honor their students' wisdom as well as their own. The fact that the crowds were impressed by Jesus's teaching demonstrates that they understood the truth he imparted, and he awakened their memory of it. Celebrated poet and civil rights activist Maya Angelou said, "I've learned that people will forget what you said, people will forget what you did, but people will never forget how you made them feel."

The Deepest Level of Communication

The mystical messiah touched people at a soul level. His *presence* was commanding. He was so identified with his spiritual nature that his students discovered *their* spiritual nature. When you speak from your heart, everyone listens, because God is speaking.

Only a small percentage of communication is verbal. The vastly greater part is nonverbal. I'm not speaking about visual cues like body posture and eye movement. The deepest nonverbal communication is energetic and spiritual.

In my seminars, I observe that when someone speaks authentically, everyone listens intently. The audience is fully engaged, hanging on every word. One who expresses from her soul touches the soul of her listeners. By contrast, when someone speaks from their head or ego, the room goes dead. The speaker is uttering words, but not saying anything meaningful. Listeners grow distracted, look at the clock, finger their phones, and head for the restroom. True presence is commanding. Lack of presence is boring and frustrating.

I saw an ad for a Korean cell phone that supposedly measures the amount of passion in the voice of the person speaking to you. This would enable you to know whether or not the other person is in love with you. I had to laugh. You don't need a machine to discern life force from its absence. We all have a built-in truth meter. When someone speaks sincerely, you know it. When someone is lying or their words are devoid of authority, you know it. The Holy Spirit is constantly guiding us to distinguish between realness and phoniness.

Christ is an experience more than an idea. You can gesture toward Christ with your intellect, but you can know Christ only with your heart. A Zen aphorism advises, "Don't mistake the finger pointing at the moon for the moon itself." The thinking mind can direct us toward healing, but only the soul mind can unite us with it. Why study about Jesus when you can know him intimately?

The Power Within You

Jesus said, "All authority has been given to me in heaven and on earth." That same authority is yours. God has given us the power to create with our minds. You have generated the entire world you see with your mind. If you like what you see, take credit for the vision you have chosen. If you do not like what you see, accept responsibility for the vision you have chosen. As long as you believe there is an external power that determines your life, you are denying the authority God has seeded within you. Nothing outside you can hurt you and nothing outside you can save you. At this moment you can command all the health, wealth, right relationships, and success your heart desires. When you know that you are an expression of God, the power that rules the universe is yours.

WHERE HEAVEN
LIVES

After Jesus was arrested, he was taken before the Sanhedrin, the board of rabbis that governed the Jewish religion. These leaders were severely threatened by this rebel who defied religious rules, publicly decried them as hypocrites, and staged a dramatic overthrow of the temple's marketplace. These men had every reason to be worried about this unabashed game changer.

Since the Romans occupied Israel, the Sanhedrin did not have the power to condemn a man. So they turned Jesus over to Pontius Pilate, the Roman governor. Pilate was also troubled by this agitator who, riding on the momentum of his growing popularity, could easily rouse the masses to revolt. Pilate asked Jesus directly, "Are you the king of the Jews?"

Jesus's answer was beyond brilliant: "My kingdom is not of this world."

The mystical messiah was pointing us to a kingdom far beyond insecure people bickering over chattels and territory. He was saying, in essence, "I am not interested in the ego games and squabbles that dominate your world. I walk in the kingdom of love. Anyone who recognizes the emptiness of the world and the riches of heaven would gladly trade a miniscule world for a mighty one; a pit of suffering for unspeakable joy."

The kingdom Jesus claimed is the proper home of every child of God. The world that teases, taunts, and binds most people cannot confine the Christ, our true nature. You deserve far more than the story the news shows you. People who constantly watch the news get depressed because the kingdom it depicts is not the world we are born to live in. Jesus was directing us to that kingdom, and gave us many hints on how to reach it.

Guidance for the Rich Man

Earlier in Christ's ministry, a wealthy young man asked him, "What must I do to enter the kingdom of heaven?" Jesus looked upon him with deep compassion and told him, "Sell all you have, give the money to the poor, and you will find treasure in heaven. Then follow me." The Bible tells us that the man grew forlorn and turned away.

Here the master was underscoring the futility of attempting to find peace by amassing the treasures of the world, "where moths and rust corrupt, and thieves break in and steal." The ego promises us that the more stuff we acquire, the happier we will be. Yet if you have ever obtained lots of possessions, you know that the more stuff you have, the more anxiety consumes you. Actor Jim Carrey said, "I think everybody should get rich and famous and do everything they dreamed of so they can see that it's not the answer."

The answer is to upgrade our goal from *objects* to *experience*. We believe that acquiring more stuff will bring us peace, when it is the choice for peace that brings us peace. *A Course in Miracles* tells us that when all you want is peace, that is all you will have. If you don't have peace, you are valuing something else more. "Follow me," did not necessarily mean that the businessman needed to join Jesus's troupe and trek with the apostles. Jesus was encouraging the man to step into Jesus's values and follow the model of inner fulfillment he demonstrated.

Don't Postpone Joy

Jesus spoke of the kingdom of heaven eighty times, and he characterized it in many ways. While many religions relegate heaven to the afterlife, Jesus regarded it as an exalted state we can enjoy *within* life. "The kingdom of heaven is at hand" means that infinite love is available right where you stand. Jesus was not a pie-in-the-sky, "suffer now and inherit paradise after you die" teacher. He did not set up a daunting series of hoops we must jump through and duties we must perform before we can be worthy of God's love. A great deal of Christ's ministry was aimed at taking back the power we have ascribed to external authorities or afterlife reward. *A Course in Miracles* asks us, "Why wait for heaven?"

Reach In, Not Out

When Jesus said, "the kingdom of heaven is within you," he was cutting away the tendency to look outside ourselves for fulfillment. We reach for happiness through a romantic partner, fancy home, prestigious job, travel to exotic places, and amassing stuff. While it's perfectly fine to have all of these and more, to really enjoy them we must keep our priorities in order. "Seek first the kingdom of heaven, and all these things shall be added unto you." When you make inner peace your first priority, whatever you need in the world will come easily and effortlessly, by grace. The universe has your back.

Heaven in the Fiber of Life

The master offered the parable of a baker who mixes a small quantity of yeast into a large batch of dough. When the bread is baked, all the dough rises because the yeast is distributed throughout it. When we integrate Spirit into the fiber of our life, all of our daily activities rise to a higher level. A little choice for well-being goes a long way. Without that fundamental intention, life is flat, brittle, and hard to digest. With it, life comes alive. As Saint Irenaeus later declared, "the glory of God is humanity fully alive."

When faith eclipses fear, miracles happen. Irma is a seventy-four-year-old woman who lives on the second story of her apartment building. One day a fire broke out in the building, and the hallway was consumed with fire and smoke. Irma had no other escape route but through the window. She said a prayer for protection and jumped off the roof with no safety net to catch her. Miraculously, Irma landed on her feet and did not fall to the ground. She was not even injured. Irma did have a safety net—the presence of a loving God.

Plant Your Seeds Wisely

Jesus also likened the kingdom of heaven to a farmer who went out to plant some seeds. Along the way, some of the seeds fell on the footpath, and they were trampled, or birds came to eat them. Others fell on rocky ground, and when they came up, they withered because of lack of moisture. Some seeds grew up among thorns that choked them out. Yet other seeds fell into fertile soil, where they developed healthily and produced abundant fruit.

Seeds in this parable represent positive, loving, visionary thoughts, words, and actions. If we drop them on the footpath where most people walk, they will be trampled by the limiting beliefs in which most of the human race is steeped. The negative, fear-based opinions of others will devour them like hungry birds. It takes sincerity of intention and a strong will not to get caught up in the maze of soul-depleting conversations and activities that dominate most people's attention.

If good ideas fall on the rocky soil of the dry intellect, they will not grow because the moisture of a loving heart is absent. The intellect dissects truth into tiny, disconnected pieces that bear little resemblance to its original wholeness. What many people call education is really a rabbit hole. You can think your way out of heaven. You can also think your way back in.

The thorny bush represents the thicket of doubt, self-criticism, and emotional upset that block out the sunlight of the presence of love. It's impossible for healing, uplifting ideas to establish themselves, grow, and bear fruit in an environment of suffocating thoughts and feelings. If you keep putting yourself down, God cannot lift you up. Give yourself a break and let the universe grow you to your fullest potential.

Ideas planted in the fertile ground of a positive mental environment will grow healthy and strong. When you meditate, pray, use affirmations, read uplifting books, watch thoughtful movies, engage in meaningful conversations, and attend uplifting classes or church services, your positive thoughts will be nurtured and your spiritual self will become your predominant identity.

Some people feel guilty about turning down invitations, relationships, or environments that drag them down. One of my coaching clients told me, "I am struggling with a mental and emotional block. I can't stand watching the news any more or engaging in gossip." I told him, "What you are calling a block is a sign of spiritual growth. To find news and gossip unattractive means that you value a higher calling." Saying "no" to a world obsessed with weirdness is a "yes" to a divine existence.

Once again, the real value of the parable reveals itself on the intrapersonal level. Other people's negative thoughts, conversations, or dysfunctions cannot drag you down unless your own thoughts match them. It is tempting to blame other people for disturbing us, when the real cause of disturbance is the self-defeating thoughts we indulge. If you are clear minded and aligned with Source energy, nothing in the world can move you. Then you have attained true spiritual mastery.

A World Beyond Trouble

Jesus was well aware of the difficulties we all face on our earthly journey. He declared, "In the world you shall have tribulation. But be of good cheer, for I have overcome the world." The physical world is built on opposites: light and dark, good and evil, life and death. Many of us feel trapped on a battleground; wherever we turn there is some threat. We spend our days fending off nasty people and situations that endanger our happiness. Yet we have the power to rise above the battleground. The master said, "My peace I give to you. Not as the world gives, but as I give." The world's peace is temporary and fleeting. God's peace is everlasting. At some point we must decide which world we will live in. When you are tired of the battleground, you seek higher ground. Jesus says to us, in effect, "Just as I found my way to well-being, so can you."

You might feel so engulfed in darkness that you believe you will never find your way to the light. That is an illusion perpetrated by fear. Sometimes the light becomes *more* available when you feel impossibly stuck. At such a point you are highly motivated to escape. Many people have found enlightenment or healing after they have gone through a dark night of the soul. They get so fed up with the life they were living that they desperately yearn for a better way. When you sincerely reach up, no matter how far you have gone down, the hand of God takes yours and lifts you beyond the world of tribulation to an experience that far transcends the physical dimension, "a peace that passes understanding."

Jesus spoke three times more of the kingdom of heaven than he did of hell. He wanted to instill within us the vision of where we are headed, rather than reinforce images of what we are growing beyond. His mission was to deliver humanity from the nasty situation we have manufactured, and set our feet on the lawns of paradise. He built a bridge from the dregs of Earth to the heart of God, and beckons us to cross it with him. Christ's kingdom was not of this world, and neither is ours.

ALL THE WAY HOME

In some of my seminars I lead a very revealing exercise. Participants pair off, and one person asks the other, "Who are you?" over and over again. People come up with all kinds of answers. *I am Susan. I am a mother. I am Todd's wife. I am forty-two years old. I am a graphic artist. I am an introvert. I am a Scorpio. I am a Raiders fan. I am ADHD.* And on and on. Eventually, after voicing many different identities, the speaker realizes, "That's who I am in the world—but there is more to me than that."

Jesus Christ knew perfectly clearly who that "more to me" was. He stepped beyond his identity as a body or personality, and recognized himself as a perfect expression of God. The tricky thing about being the Son of God is that it is difficult to explain your identity to others who believe they are trapped in time and space. It's even harder to convince them that they, too, are immortal. So the master made statements like, "I am the way, the truth, and the life," "I and the Father are one," and "no one comes to the Father except by me." Such metaphysical statements left his listeners, then and now, scratching our heads trying to figure out what he really meant.

Those lofty declarations are Christ's most important teachings because through them he was pointing us toward our own exalted nature. Parables about farming, weddings, and cooking were metaphorical guides to teach us how to live in the world. Jesus also wanted us to live *beyond* the world. All interpersonal training leads to intrapersonal insight, which culminates in transpersonal awakening. Jesus Christ is a role model of who we become when we remember our true self. He never said, "I am a divine being and you are not." "You are not" is a story the sleeping mind conjured. The spiritual path is about peeling away mistaken identities to reveal our inherent glory. Our ultimate destiny is not to keep learning lessons in the world. Our ultimate destiny is to transcend the world.

Let us now focus on some of Jesus's most penetrating transpersonal teachings, that we may see the universe through his eyes.

"I and the Father are one... Whoever has seen me has seen the Father."

A ray of sunlight contains all the attributes of the sun. What is in the sun is in the ray. You cannot split the ray off from the sun. It would have no purpose or existence. If you know the ray, you know the sun.

Jesus knew his true self to be the same as God. He rose beyond body identification and the limits imposed by his human intellect and physical experience. Jesus's mind was and is the mind of God. His sense of "I am" expanded to be all that God is. What's true of God is true of Christ and is true of you. The Apostle Paul implored us, "Let this mind be in you, which was also in Christ Jesus."

Paul's next statement is even more stunning:

> Who, being in the form of God,
> thought it not robbery to be equal with God.

This bold declaration gives us all permission to be equal to God. It is not too presumptuous to claim our divine nature. We might believe we are arrogant to say, "I am one with God," as if we are somehow stealing God's identity. You cannot steal what is already yours. You cannot fake your true self. You do not diminish what you are by declaring what you are. When you claim your divine identity, you reinforce it. When you own something, you inherit all of its rights, powers, and privileges. When you acknowledge that God lives in you as you, you are fulfilling God's purpose and your own. You are not a crook. The divine estate is already yours.

"I am the way, the truth, and the life."

The key to understanding this mighty statement is to know who was the "I" Christ referred to. Jesus did not think of himself as a person. He thought of himself as a living spirit. He identified himself with the attributes of God, not the attributes of people. We can do the same.

When an extraordinarily talented person is fully dedicated to his or her craft, they merge with it. The part disappears into the whole, and they *become* their vocation. We might say that Beethoven *is* impassioned music, and Nikola Tesla *is* visionary science. Many people consider Meryl Streep to be the world's greatest living actress because she disappears into her roles and becomes the person she is playing. You can't separate the wave from the ocean; the existence of one implies the other.

Jesus was so immersed in life force that he became it. We can use Jesus's personality as a focal or starting point, but we must sail beyond it. Why keep your boat moored in a bay when you have access to the entire ocean? Christ was urging us, "Walk the path I have walked, and you will find the treasure I have found." At some point we cease seeking God, and we become God.

In the Hindu epic Ramayana, the monkey Hanuman is the servant of Ram, the incarnation of God. Hanuman tells Ram, "When I forget who I am, I serve you. When I remember who I am, I *am* you." Jesus Christ became the God he served, modeling the evolution we all undergo.

"No one comes to the Father except by me."

The "me" Jesus refers to is universal. You can absolutely come to the Father by way of Jesus Christ. If you are a Christian who has accepted Jesus Christ as your savior, you have chosen wisely. He can take you all the way home. A friend of mine wrote a song, "You Can't Go Wrong with Jesus." So it is. A purer representation of God has never walked the Earth. If you follow the precepts he taught and live the life he prescribed, your heart will be at peace and you will arrive in heaven.

There are other personalities that can also take you to the Father. If you have faith in a guru or spiritual master as an incarnation of God, that person can guide you to salvation. When people were healed in Jesus's presence, he told them, "Your faith has made you whole." Likewise, it is your faith that reveals God, whether through Jesus or through another divine teacher. The Christ is too big to be contained in one person. Great souls on many different spiritual paths unite humanity with our Source. No religion has a monopoly on truth or owns God more than another. When you input a destination into a GPS, it shows you several different possible routes. In the end, the road you take to your destination is less important than that you arrive where you want to go.

"He that is in me is greater than he that is in the world... It is not I, but the Father within me that does the work."

Any truly talented person acknowledges that their gifts proceed from a higher source. No one invents their own greatness; they step into it. If they think they are the source of their blessings, they are on an ego trip to nowhere. Good things pour to the world from God *through* people. Jesus knew that he was the vessel through which God accomplished the results. He emptied himself of ego and allowed Higher Power to move the world through him.

If you feel tired or burnt out, a part of you believes that you are doing the work. You labor under undue responsibility. When you are in your right mind, your activity in the world is a co-creation between you and God, and you are not fatigued, but empowered. You are wise to pray, "Use me as You would." Then your heavenly Source arranges all the details. It places you with the perfect people in the perfect situations at the perfect time for the perfect purpose. Miracles happen because you allow the Father to work through you.

Jesus was clear on where his energy and blessings came from. When we are so clear, we will perform even greater miracles.

It is Written

Claiming to be the Son of God poses a threat to those who believe they are not. A world adamant to defend limits must get rid of anyone who proves that we have none. Many people have been crucified in one way or another for identifying themselves with Spirit. Yet Jesus was uncompromising in his mission to awaken humanity to our spiritual nature.

> The Jews answered Him, "For your works we do not stone you, but for blasphemy; and because you, being a man, make yourself out to be God." Jesus answered them, "Has it not been written in your Law, 'I said, you are gods?'"

Jesus was referring to Psalm 82:6: *"I said, 'You are gods; you are all sons of the Most High.'"* We have been taught that humility lies in admitting our unworthiness. But to identify ourselves as unworthy is the ultimate arrogance, as we refute the perfection in which we were created. There is far more to us than our ego and errors. Behind our human dramas, greatness lives. Jesus had the courage to make a stand for the majesty he shared with his Father, and he calls us to do the same.

Let Not Your Heart Be Troubled

Christ spoke these final words to his disciples:

> My peace I give you. I do not give
> to you as the world gives.

> Do not let your hearts be troubled
> and do not be afraid.

> Arise, let us leave this place.

Jesus takes us by the hand and guides us from a world of mayhem to one of deep tranquility. We cease to regard ourselves as outside of love's embrace, and we are restored. Our long, burdensome journey leads us to the door of the mansion we left in search of something better. We are saved by the stunning realization that we carried our good within us even as we searched elsewhere. All of our experiences have led us to where we now stand. Heaven is ours because we choose it above all else.

BEEN THERE,
DONE THAT

Much of Christianity revolves around the crucifixion of Jesus Christ. The cross upon which he died has become the symbol of the religion. Was this the master's intention, or is it the result of people filtering a love story through the lens of fear? The time has come for us to rethink what Jesus stands for, and how he wants us to remember him. Does he want us to continue to replay the crucifixion over and over again by our own bloodletting? Or does he want us to move on to the resurrection?

In *A Course in Miracles*, Jesus describes the crucifixion as "the last useless journey." He urges us to avoid taking up the old rugged cross. This advice will likely raise the hackles of anyone who ascribes redeeming value to the blood of the lamb. If you have been taught that Jesus's death brings you life, you may be shocked to consider that he does not recommend crucifixion as a spiritual path. It takes a courageous thinker to question if suffering really buys redemption.

The teaching value of the crucifixion shines when Jesus said, "Father, forgive them, for they know not what to do." Here the mystical messiah modeled ultimate forgiveness. He was stripped, whipped, publicly humiliated, tortured, and brutally murdered—the worst possible treatment a human being can experience. Yet he found it in his heart to forgive his assailants. This extraordinary act puts our own sense of victimization in stunning perspective. Suddenly, your sister not inviting you to Thanksgiving dinner seems quite paltry in comparison. If Jesus could forgive what happened to him, we can certainly let go of far more menial mistreatment.

Some metaphysical teachers say that Jesus consciously chose to undergo the crucifixion because his dramatic death would cause people to more sharply remember his life and teachings. Maybe so. Yet there have been many other spiritual giants, like Moses, Buddha, Mohammed, and Confucius, whose deaths were gentler, and they have also influenced the world in monumental ways.

At the early stages of our spiritual journey, we require strong contrast to get our attention and prompt us to learn our lessons. If we are deeply asleep, we need a potent wake-up call, like an alarm clock that gets progressively louder until you can't ignore it. As we advance on our spiritual path, we require less striking contrast, and our lessons become lighter and gentler. Our evolution becomes more about inner processing than putting out fires. Perhaps the teaching behind the crucifixion speaks to one stage of our growth, and when we no longer find

BEEN THERE, DONE THAT

value in Jesus's suffering or our own, we graduate to a subtler level of education. In *A Course in Miracles' Manual for Teachers*, Jesus tells us that we can be healed of any disease when we realize, "I have no use for this." Could we be healed of the burden of personal crucifixion when we rise up and say, "I have no use for this?"

I heard a Christian criticize a famous minister who invites his congregants to live a prosperous, joyful life. The critic cited a long list of Christ's disciples, saints, and martyrs who died grisly deaths, often by persecution and torture. I wonder if the critic realized how much he was glorifying suffering. We don't believe what we find evidence for; we find evidence for what we believe. We can prove anything we believe will serve us. A far larger number of devout Christians have died natural deaths. As I have noted, you can argue for the value of suffering, and you can also make a case for well-being. I prefer door number two.

Over the centuries, over three hundred Christian stigmatists have spontaneously bled from the palms of their hands and other points on their body equivalent to where Jesus was impaled on the cross. If Jesus was pierced with spikes through his wrists, the common method of Roman crucifixion, why do most stigmatists bleed from the palms of their hands? Could it be that belief plays a greater part in suffering than we know? Could the martyrs have been less exercising the Christian faith, and more exercising faith in martyrdom? If you and I see ourselves as martyrs in any way, could we choose to release ourselves and live a more joyful life? In the movie *Straight Talk*, Dolly Parton plays a radio talk show psychologist. When she receives a call from a woman steeped in a martyr complex, she advises the caller to get off the cross, for somebody needs the wood.

Is There Life After Drama?

Five centuries before Christ walked the earth, the Greeks invented the drama. An actor goes through a challenge or a tragedy and emerges purged. In watching a drama, we vicariously walk through the protagonist's journey. When the hero wins his or her battle or gains a lesson, release, or redemption, we experience a catharsis, as if we have gone through the same experience. Watching dramas helps us work out our own fears and conflicts without going through the physical process ourselves.

The same kind of cleansing occurs in dreams. If you have a nightmare and then awaken from it, you pass through the experience on the subtle plane without having to undergo it on the physical plane. Your dream character does the work for you.

The world that seems so real is a drama playing out in our mind. When we see a character (seemingly out there, but really in here) undergo a difficult experience or enjoy a newfound freedom, we gain the experience without having to struggle through it personally. The Jesus character in our dream masterfully enacted the tragedy and the resolution. He walked through death, the fear we all share, and he emerged alive, the hope we all share.

The Great Realization

We are told that Jesus died for our sins. But Christ came to *undo* guilt, not reinforce it. He spent his ministry forgiving people whom others regarded as sinners. If the master's ministry was about purging the world of guilt, why would the culmination of his mission lay guilt on all humanity, unto eternity?

There is a deeper metaphysical understanding of the notion that Jesus took the sins of the world upon himself. Jesus stepped into the illusion of the world that we all share, so he could help free us from it. He chose to enter into a physical body, have a human experience, die through crucifixion, forgive his murderers, and resurrect himself as a teaching that we, too, are greater than our material circumstances. He took on the karma of the world to demonstrate that grace supersedes karma. The crucifixion would have no purpose if Jesus hadn't proclaimed forgiveness and then rose from the grave. Those two achievements represent the triumph over victimization, suffering, and death, from which we all desperately yearn to be released. Jesus participated in the dream of the world so he could help wake us up from it along with him. He came into a domain where people believe in sin so he could liberate us from that self-defeating belief.

When John the Baptist met Jesus, he declared, "Behold the lamb of God who takes away the sin of the world." Many theologians interpret this statement to indicate that Jesus was a sacrificial lamb; he absorbed the sins of humanity and purged them through his death. There is a far lighter interpretation.

I used to live on a property that had a pasture of sheep. Dee and I took great delight in watching the young lambs play. We discovered the lambs to be the sweetest, gentlest, and most innocent of creatures, models of ease, playfulness, and contentment. Jesus as the lamb of God guided humanity to God not through his murder, but through his innocence. He took away the sins of the world by teaching that our true self doesn't have any. The surface mind makes sin real and then wipes it out. A deeper mind pierces beyond the veneer of sin and beholds only innocence.

The Power Behind the Cross

If crucifixion is not on the menu for our healing, why is the cross powerful? Are we fooling ourselves by topping off churches, wearing crucifix pendants, marking graves, and fending off vampires? The cross is powerful not for its form or historical role, but for our belief in it. The real strength of the cross, like any symbol, is in our mind. Our faith in the cross makes it a valid spiritual tool. We could just as easily be energized or protected by the symbol of the Jewish star, or the crescent moon of Islam, or the Zen image of waves rippling out from a central point. Jesus's statement, "According to your faith let it be done to you," applies as much to the cross as it does to any other element of life.

The fact that the cross's power is a result of our belief does not diminish its effectiveness. It is a permission slip by which we grant ourselves access to Higher Power. If you believe in the cross or any image, it can open the door to miracles. The power of Christ is available to you by any route you to take to connect with it. Eventually we must grow beyond the belief in external objects as sources of good or ill, and recognize that all the power we could ever want or need has already been seeded within us. Christ lives in our mind and heart far more than in the image of the crucifix.

Meeting Christ on Higher Ground

Years ago I gave up watching intense dramas. I find no reward in seeing anyone suffer or fight as a means of entertainment. Many movies and books focus on sorrows more than the redemption. There was a movie about the life of Christ that fixated almost exclusively on his torment. A movie critic titled his review, "Gory, Gory, Hallelujah." I relate to Jesus as an affirmation of love, life, and hope, not the victim of torture. He is a living spirit far more than a body. If Jesus returned today, he would not repeat his crucifixion, and neither need you. Been there, done that. If you received such horrid treatment from a place you visited, would you go back for more? The world has seen enough models of torture; now it desperately needs models of healing. We are free to crucify ourselves, and we are also free to get off the cross. Christ calls us to learn from his experience and meet him on higher ground.

Just as Jesus did away with the tables of the money changers in the great temple, he might remove the crosses from today's churches, and replace them with images of the risen Christ, arms not spread in agony, but open to embrace us. He would affirm that our gift to the world is our joy, not our blood. Then, when we go to church and hear the minister tell us, "God is love," the image on the wall behind the preacher will mirror freedom from pain, not its glorification.

36

FREE AT LAST

On the third day after the crucifixion, two women went to Jesus's tomb to anoint the body. To their astonishment, the body was not there. While the women were puzzling over the absence of Jesus's body, two men in radiate attire stood beside them. They were angels. One asked the women, "Why do you look for the living among the dead?"

We might ask ourselves the same question whenever we look for life where there is none. We live devoid of passion not because life is absent, but because we are searching for the living among the dead. We confuse the spirit with the form, and seek eternality in the changing. We make objects our gods, rather than recognizing the God that reaches us through the objects.

The angel's question is important for anyone who has lost a loved one. While we grieve over the end of their body, they were never their body at all. They inhabited their body and animated it, but they were not limited to it. Our loved ones are living spirits who soar far beyond the physical plane. If we want to know them, we must seek them where they are, not where they vacated. Even while we rue their loss, our dear ones stand by our side, whispering in our ear: *Don't look for me in the grave or the urn. I am no longer in my body. Now I live in your heart.*

This liberating lesson extrapolates to any element of our life that once brought us vitality, but no longer does. A relationship, job, spiritual teacher or group, health regime, hobby, or living situation used to stimulate us immensely. Yet over time the life force has waned, and now we are bored and simply going through the motions. What once was a home and hearth has become an empty shell. We perform the rituals, but our heart is not in them. We want to move on, but we fear to let go.

At such a moment we stand at a crossroads bearing two signposts: the dead past or the vital present and future. Which path will you follow? Why are you holding on to what no longer empowers you? Why do you look for the living among the dead?

Endings Are Beginnings

Jesus Christ rising from the tomb provides a metaphor for a process we all go through. When something dies, something else is born. When something disappears, something new appears. When something limited ends, something unlimited is released. This dynamic applies not just to the death of the body, but to anything that ends. Every ending also marks a beginning. All genuine spiritual teachers agree on one truth: *There is no death.* There is only life, which keeps showing up in new and different forms.

Stephen Levine, who spent much of his life working with people who were passing over, wrote a book with a penetrating title: *Who Dies?* The short answer is: The body, the ego, and the form die, all of which are insubstantial in the face of the spirit. From limited vision, the body is real and the spirit is a dream. From expanded vision, the spirit is real and the body is a dream. My teacher said, "When a child is born, people smile and the angels weep. When someone dies, people cry and the angels rejoice."

Nothing is born when the body dies. We simply return to who we have been all along. We awaken from the strange dream architected by the world, and we go home.

Relationship Resurrection

If it's hard to understand physical resurrection, we might find it easier to observe resurrection in relationships. We have all gone through some kind of breakup, divorce, or the end of a friendship or business relationship. Or a family member may shun us. Most of these transitions are painful, as we value the good things about the relationship, and we wish it had continued. If we fell in love, we wish we could have sustained that wonderful feeling.

Yet the death of one form gave way to something better. In retrospect you can see how the relationship served you while you were in it, and also how it served you by its ending. You got into the relationship for the wrong reasons, or you and your partner grew apart, or you learned the lesson you entered the relationship to gain, or you completed your soul contract, or there was some other reason the relationship could not continue. You grew through the experience and you are wiser for it. Perhaps you learned to be more honest, trust and follow your intuition, communicate more directly, set healthier boundaries, or be kinder to yourself. You graduated from the relationship with many spiritual gifts you did not own when you entered it.

Many people feel guilty after a divorce because they did not fulfill the vow, "'til death do us part." But defining death only as the death of a body is quite shortsighted. Relationships die as surely as bodies die. If you separated because the relationship died, death has done you part. To stay in an unloving, unhealthy, or abusive relationship after it has died serves no one. An old Chinese adage advises, "When your horse dies, get off." Many people try to continue to ride the relationship after the horse has died. Seeking life where there is none is frustrating and debilitating, and holds you back from moving on to the next rewarding step on your relationship journey.

The highest purpose of a relationship ending is to achieve resurrection. Ascend out of the carcass of the relationship and reclaim your happy, glowing self. Your spirit may have been stifled in a relationship, but it did not die. It remains golden and intact, waiting for you to regain it and live your richest life, far beyond the one you knew when you partnered. If you blame yourself for a relationship ending, you have an opportunity to forgive yourself and recognize your innocence. You did the best you could with what you knew. Now you know more.

In truth, relationships don't die. Love is forever. If someone passed away or left your life, the love you experienced with that person is just as real and alive as it ever was. The expression of love is just taking a different form. Love is available through many channels, not just that one. If the person has passed on, they are available for you to connect and communicate with them at a higher frequency. If the person is still alive and you ended on bad terms, you have a magnificent opportunity to do your inner work and achieve healing with them, at least within your own heart. If you hold resentment, regret, anger, or guilt, the relationship is still raging within you, calling you to release the painful emotions and choose love instead. That will happen for you and your partner, someday somehow. You may or may not see that manifestation in this physical life, but it will surely happen on your spiritual journey. *A Course in Miracles* promises, "A happy outcome to all things is sure."

Soul Relationships

Relationships happen between souls, not bodies. The bodies may serve as vehicles for the expression of soul, but bodies by themselves are incapable of relationships. By analogy, cars do not have relationships with each other. They are machines. Their drivers may have relationships, but not cars. Cars and bodies are inert. Souls are expressions of life. Our lives have meaning only when we recognize that we are spiritual beings and we relate to each other as rays of the divine.

If you define yourself as a body only, and likewise your partner, you are in for a rough ride. While it appears that bodies love each other, it is really the people who inhabit the bodies that share the love. One day your bodies will change and disappear. Then what will be left? The answer is the secret of the resurrection: Only love endures. Only love remains. Only love is real.

When a disciple asked Jesus if he should attend his father's funeral, Jesus answered, "Let the dead bury the dead," meaning that bodies bury bodies, but the spirits of both the living and the apparently dead enjoy a reality far beyond what the bodies are doing. Jesus advised the disciple, "Instead, follow me and proclaim the kingdom of God," meaning, "Place your attention on where life is, and celebrate the presence of love that transcends the material world."

The Final Step to Freedom

All beliefs serve a purpose for a while, but then they must be transcended. You must grow beyond the way you think it is. You might participate in a religion or political party, follow a guru, or maintain a cultural identity, ethical practice, or diet. While such regimes can be helpful, there is a bigger belief system than the one you have known. I know many people who were raised in a religion their parents forced upon them, or they believed in. Later they found the religion stifling, or they no longer agreed with its dogma. When that person attempted to leave the fold, they felt guilty, or members of the religion tried to force them to stay. Eventually these people found the courage to go on to live a more expanded life, and they achieved resurrection.

Some elements of religion and gurus are very close to God. If you follow them, they serve as doorways to heaven. But you don't want to stand in the doorway forever; you gain the real reward when you keep going to enter the room where the doorway leads. An Indian sage said, "If a thorn is stuck in your foot, you can use another thorn to remove it. But then you must throw both thorns away." Your religion, spiritual practice, or belief system is a good thorn that helps you remove a bad one.

But it is still a thorn. The day will come when you will leave all thorns behind, and live free.

The End of Doubt

We are told that after the resurrection Jesus appeared to the disciples in his physical body. When the doubting disciple Thomas questioned if this apparition was real, Jesus invited him to place his fingers into the wounds where he had been pierced for his crucifixion. When Thomas did so and felt Jesus's flesh, he knew that this was really Jesus, and his doubts dissolved.

Jesus manifested a physical body in order to convince the disciples—and us—that he was still very much alive in spite of the fact that he had been pronounced dead. This was a dramatic teaching to give the disciples—and us—faith that there is reality beyond our material journey. Jesus's physical appearance was an act of compassion, like his whole life, to meet human beings where we live and reach us within the world to help us transcend the world.

A good teacher does not ask a student to jump all the way from hell to heaven in one leap. In very rare cases, this occurs spontaneously. In most scenarios, we need to ascend the staircase to heaven one step at a time. Lofty spiritual teachings come to the world through books, movies, music, and art. God reaches us through the forms we find familiar, hold dear, and can relate to. The noblest purpose of literature, education, and entertainment is to stimulate humanity to look up to a higher truth. Everything else is filler or, as Shakespeare said, prologue.

Faith and doubt are constantly vying for the dominant position in our mind. They cannot coexist in any given moment;

you must make a choice. You can accelerate the predominance of faith by contrasting how faith and doubt each feel. Faith is uplifting and empowering, while doubt is debilitating. Recognizing this crucial difference will help establish your higher vision rather than spinning in old, painful cycles spun by fear.

Many of us feel entombed by an oppressive relationship, meaningless job, unhappy living situation, physical condition, or a crazy world. None of these situations have the power to bind us. We keep ourselves stuck by clinging to what was, rather than embracing what is, or what could be. We achieve resurrection by changing our mind. We must replace thoughts of smallness, lack, and victimization with the awareness of grandiosity, supply, and empowerment. Then we escape the tomb that once encased us. People who come to look for us in the tomb will not find us. We have moved on. Miguel Cervantes, author of the beloved *Don Quixote*, said, "Never look for this year's birds in last year's nests." In his resurrection, Jesus left his old nest behind, and in our resurrection, so do we.

THE SECRET OF THE
SECOND COMING

I sometimes drive past a church that displays a huge pink and blue neon sign proclaiming, "Jesus is Coming." My friend Albert sits glued to his television, watching the news for signs that the end of the world is near, when Christ will descend to initiate the rapture. At the Passover meal, Jews leave an empty seat for the messianic prophet Elijah to join the gathering. They pour him a cup of wine and open the door for him to enter. In one way or another, we are all hoping and waiting for a savior to redeem the world from the hardships that plague humanity.

Yet for all these noble visions and rituals, there is a flaw that keeps redemption at a distance. There will not be a second coming of Christ because the first one never ended. The man Jesus came and went, but the Christ, his true nature and ours, lives forever. Christ is just as much with us now as when he walked in the flesh, as he always will be. The Book of Hebrews declares, "Jesus Christ is the same yesterday, today, and forever." Jesus affirmed, "Before Abraham was, I am."

The presence of Christ is not an event in time. It is a reality far beyond time. The master promised, "I will be with you until the end of time." The end of time is not linear. There will not come a day when time runs out. The end of time is an event in consciousness. At any moment we have the ability to rise beyond time. When we leave our ego behind and claim our reality as spiritual beings, Christ is here to welcome us home.

The real second coming—or more precisely the continuation and consummation of the first—will be the awakening of humanity to the Christ that lives in all of us. Jesus is still waiting for us to live the message he delivered two thousand years ago. When we have mastered "love your neighbor as yourself," he will give us the next lesson. Until then, we have our homework to do.

Many great teachers have brought the Christ presence to the world. They come in all religions and no religion. If God were limited to one messenger, avenues to reach humanity would be severely curtailed. Restricting revelation to Jesus would be like choosing English as the only language that affords communication. Speakers of all languages enjoy the same capacity to connect. The message far outshines the messenger.

While many await a savior, he will not arrive again as a man. The second coming is not a body, but a consciousness. The messiah is a state of mind, the flower of all spiritual evolution. When humanity owns its Christed nature, Jesus's mission will be complete.

Jesus invites you to join him as a redeemer of humanity. But first you must rise beyond the belief that Jesus has something you do not also embody, and he is someplace you are not. We talk about the passion of the Christ as his crucifixion. But his true passion is to awaken the Christ in everyone he touches. He wants us to walk by his side and share his purpose as the light of the world. If you are waiting for Jesus to show up before you can be the light of the world, you miss his fundamental teaching. We must each be a lighthouse *before* we see Jesus in the flesh. Then we *become* Christ in the flesh.

Proselytizers ask, "Have you been saved?" Their idea of being saved is to join their church. But the church of Christ spans far beyond a building or an organization. Real salvation is liberation from an identity that defines you as separate from God. You are not separate from Jesus, Christ, or God, which are all aspects of yourself. Worshipping Jesus Christ is an interim step to acknowledging the Christ in you. When you can say with equal authority, "I and the Father are one," you are home.

From the Body to the Spirit

One of the ways we distance ourselves from healing is to get fixated on the body of Jesus rather than experiencing the presence of the Christ. We designate form as the object instead of celebrating the energy that animates the form. Some spiritual or religious people criticize others who pay too much attention to their bodies. If someone intensively focuses on clothing and makeup, body building, cosmetic surgery, or desperately trying to look young when they are old, we may consider them self-absorbed or vain. Yet we make the same mistake when we limit Jesus to his physical form. He is far more than that. He is a living spirit. No lesser definition honors him. You can't put a genie back in a bottle, and you can't stuff Christ into a body.

267

If Jesus Christ showed up in the flesh today, I would drop everything to go and bask in his presence. You might do the same. Yet he does show up in the flesh, but not in one unique person. He shows up in everyone we encounter. Every soul contains the Christ essence, or Buddha nature, or Krishna song, or Hebrew *neshama*, divine spirit. To access that glorious presence, we must pierce beyond the illusion that we are physical beings only, our "Earth suits." We must shift our identity from the fleeting to the eternal. *A Course in Miracles* reminds us, "When you meet anyone, remember it is a holy encounter."

A Hindu story tells of a fellow who trekked with his dog to the peaks of the Himalayas, where he intensely searched for the portal to heaven. After many tribulations with his faithful companion at his side, he found the door to paradise. There the gatekeeper told him that he had earned the right to enter heaven, but he would have to leave his dog behind. The fellow thought about the invitation and told the gatekeeper, "I am not going anywhere, including heaven, without my dog." Hearing that, the dog revealed its identity as the god Krishna, and both entered heaven together.

There are two morals of this story: First, the pets and people we love are God in disguise. Some people call dogs "angels with fur." Every living being carries the essence of the divine, no matter their appearance. God peeks at us through the eyes of everyone we meet, and touches our heart through theirs.

The second moral is that we all get into heaven together, or not at all. You can't get saved without recognizing everyone's right to be saved. When redemption comes, no one gets left behind. If you leave anyone outside the right to be healed, you deny yourself the same right. Any heaven that excludes anyone is not the real heaven. We have all suffered together, and we will all escape together. The gate of heaven is wide enough for all humanity to enter.

The End of Waiting

While you are waiting for Jesus to show up, he is waiting for you to show up. There is no delay in the divine; people have invented the idea of delay to avoid the perfection present now. Another name for Jesus is "Emmanuel," which means "God is with us." It doesn't mean, "God was with us, and then departed," or "One day God will be with us." It means God is with us. Now. Let us not put off until a future time what is already wholly and holy given. While we may wait for a special baby to be born as Christ, he is born through every baby. If Jesus comes in the form of a person, that person will point you to your own Christed self.

We need to move the second coming of Christ from a sense of anticipation, to a sense of celebration. We need to quit looking up, and start looking in. Jesus will not descend from the clouds, but emerge from the mist that shrouds hearts consumed with fear. A Course in Miracles tells us, "You are not saved *from* anything, but you are saved *for* glory." Our mission is to give Christ a venue to walk the Earth again through us.

During his sojourn on Earth, Jesus gave us crucial clues as to how he has been with us, and how he will come again.

I was hungry and you fed me. I was thirsty and you gave me a drink. I was a stranger and you took me in. I was naked and you clothed me. I was sick and you cared for me. I was in prison and you visited me . . . Whatever you did for one of the least of my brothers, you did for me.

Whenever we treat someone with compassion and kindness, we are invoking the presence of Christ on Earth. In the introduction to this book, I listed the many Jesuses that people relate to, from the religious Jesus to the political Jesus to the family Jesus to the mystical Jesus. Now I introduce the final Jesus: the universal Jesus. This Christ lives beyond gender, age, nationality, race, or religion. This is the Christ that shows up whenever we help relieve another person's suffering in the slightest way. When we treat each other as the Christ, we invoke his presence. Jesus goes wherever he is welcome. Through our Christlike deeds we welcome Jesus back to Earth, and the second coming is accomplished.

Becoming Christ

Humanity needs a living vision of our highest potential. Jesus Christ fills that role. His superpowers do not underscore our frailties by contrast, but instead they highlight the strengths we have yet to claim. Every biblical reference to Jesus points to our hidden identity as a spiritual giant. Every miracle he performed, you can perform. Every healing he achieved is a healing you deserve, and can bestow upon others. God walking the Earth as Jesus Christ symbolizes God walking the Earth as you. Jesus was humanity's loftiest possibility made flesh, the vision of who we will become when we remember who we are.

You Rock

At the height of his ministry, Jesus dispatched the disciples to go forth, teach, and heal. When they returned, they told of their encounters with people who conjectured who Jesus was. Some Judeans thought Jesus was John the Baptist; others, the prophet Elijah; and others, Jeremiah. Finally Jesus asked the disciples, "And who do you say I am?" Peter thought deeply and answered, "You are the Christ, the son of the living God."

Jesus, well pleased, placed his hands on Peter's shoulders, looked him firmly in the eyes, and replied, "This was not revealed to you by flesh and blood . . . You are the rock upon which I will build my church."

The disciples represent your divine attributes that go out into the world and testify to a greater truth. The people of Judea, guessing about who Jesus was, represent the scattered thoughts of the intellect, attempting to understand holiness with the rational mind, which can point at truth but never capture it.

Peter symbolizes the part of your mind that recognizes the presence of Christ. This knowing has not arrived as a result of a train of thought; it runs deeper than the intellect can fathom. Only higher vision reveals higher truth. When Peter acknowledged Jesus as the messiah, you are acknowledging your Christed nature. The part of you that recognizes the Christ *is* the Christ. It takes one to know one. The scene is an epic depiction of self-awakening.

Just as Jesus promised to build his church on Peter's deep knowing, God will build your life on your faith. Here again we must understand that the real church is not a religion. It is a state of consciousness. Jesus did not intend to start a religion. He intended to deliver truth to the world. People form religions in an attempt to capture and sustain truth. In a way they do; many pure elements within Christianity remain true to Christ's vision. Yet corruption creeps into all religions and distorts the original message. Jesus spent a significant part of his ministry exposing the hypocrisy that had infiltrated the Jewish religion. If he were to return today, he would do the same for Christianity. The master said, "The gates of hell will not prevail against my church." The gates of hell have indeed prevailed against many churches because they have become misaligned with the intention of their founder. Yet the gates of hell cannot touch a pure state of mind. If you remember that Christ's real church is the consciousness he attained, you will rise above the trappings of ego, and renew his presence on Earth through your own.

From Discipleship to Mastery

When reading about the deeds of Jesus, we are prone to identify with the disciples sitting at his feet, absorbing his empowering words. Now I invite you to an even more majestic vision: *being* Jesus uttering life-changing truth. To the worldly mind, becoming Jesus is an outrageous assertion. To the divine mind, it is the only assertion worth accepting. To identify as a disciple of Christ is noble. To identify as Christ is self-realization.

The mystical messiah is not a man who walked the earth two thousand years ago. It is the part of your mind that calls you to awaken from within. As long as you expect liberation to come through a person outside yourself, you miss the essential element of your soul that you were born to uncover. Jesus does not want to be marginalized as a disowned projection of your own divinity. He wants you to discover the elements of himself that you already own, and *are*. He wants to release you from needing him, and empower you by *claiming* him. He seeks not your worship, but your *worthship*. While many look up to Jesus, few look within to the Christ. The one to whom billions bow did not come to be ensconced as an icon, but to reflect as a mirror. He is an idea more than a person. Bodies are limited to a point in time and space. Ideas are everywhere at once. The idea that Jesus came to express is far more important than the form that came and went.

A traditional hymn extols, "What a friend we have in Jesus." Indeed we do. Yet Plato said, "True friendship can occur only among equals." If we are to be a friend to Jesus, and he to us, we cannot allow idolatry to quake the common ground we share with him. The consummation of our relationship with Jesus Christ is to look directly into his eyes and call him not just master, but brother. The disciple becomes the master; the seeker, the sought; the lost, the found; and the human, God.

If accepting your Christed nature is too great a stretch, then continue to raise your eyes to Jesus. We must each advance at the pace most comfortable to us. Yet one day we will trade adoration for self-knowledge; reverence for equality; idolatry for divinity.

Jesus Christ has not cornered the market on godliness; holiness is equally and fairly distributed. When we become what Jesus became, the Bible has achieved its purpose. The great saga, we finally recognize, is our own. Then there will be no need to worship a God outside of us and over us. We discover that the distant God we sought to please lived within us all along, as us, through us, with us, and for us. Then we will all walk in divine dignity, and leave behind the epic story that brought us to the great and final liberation.

ACKNOWLEDGMENTS

Jesus Christ is a guiding light in my life. To me he is real, available, ever-present, and eternally kind and compassionate. His essence reflects divine wisdom and the pure love of God. I consider Jesus the role model of mastery, a channel for healing, and the exemplar of God walking the earth as a human being. I thank Jesus Christ for modeling grace and helping me in ways far beyond I can help myself. His blessing to humanity goes beyond words and measure.

Many brilliant and loving teachers have introduced me to the mystical messiah and revealed his divine aspects to me. I acknowledge them in the order I met them: Ram Dass, Hilda Charlton, the Ascended Masters, Mother Mary, St. Francis of Assisi, Franco Zeffirelli, St. Teresa of Lisieux, Ken Keyes, Rev. Willard Fuller, Dr. Eric Butterworth, Ernest Holmes, *A Course in Miracles*, Carla Gordan, Mary, Serena, the Guides, Joel Goldsmith, Neville Goddard, Florence Scovel Shinn, Joseph Murphy, Reverend Ike, and Joel Osteen. All of these master teachers have shined the light of Christ into my life and the world.

My beloved partner Dee demonstrates Christlike kindness to me and others every day. She supports me in the highest way to bring good things to the world through my writing and other teachings. Her thoughtful feedback and comments empower me, the material, and all readers.

Thanks once again to Natascha Bohmann for her impeccable proofreading. Elena Karoumpali continues to amaze me with her outstanding cover graphics. Isabel Robalo has graced the interior design with extraordinary talent and care.

I honor every soul who has found a sincere, heartful connection with Jesus and the Christ energy, by whatever name we call it. Such dedicated individuals live the teachings of Jesus by being kind to other human beings, maintaining an open heart, praying for people and the world, and giving healing. Christ walks with us, through us, as us. We are blessed beyond words.

About the Author

ALAN COHEN, M.A., holds degrees in psychology and human organizational development.

He is the author of 30 popular inspirational books, including the best-selling *A Course in Miracles Made Easy* and the award-winning *A Deep Breath of Life*. He is a contributing writer for the #1 *New York Times* best-selling series *Chicken Soup for the Soul*, and he is featured in the book *101 Top Experts Who Help Us Improve Our Lives*. His books have been translated into 32 foreign languages.

Alan has taught at Montclair State College, Omega Institute for Holistic Studies, and en*Theos Academy for Optimal Living.

He is a featured presenter in the award-winning documentary *Finding Joe*, celebrating the teachings of Joseph Campbell. His work has been presented on CNN and Oprah.com and in *USA Today*, *The Washington Post*, and *Huffington Post*. His monthly column *From the Heart* is published in magazines internationally.

Alan is the founder and Director of the Foundation for Holistic Life Coaching. He presents programs on themes of life mastery, spiritual development, and vision psychology.

For information on Alan Cohen's books, seminars, life coach training, videos, and audio recordings, visit:

www.alancohen.com

Facebook:
www.facebook.com/AlanCohenAuthor

Twitter:
www.twitter.com/alanhcohen

Instagram:
www.instagram.com/alancohenauthor

YouTube:
www.youtube.com/user/Cowinn327

Learn More with Alan Cohen

If you have enjoyed and benefited from *The Mystical Messiah*, you may want to deepen your understanding and inspiration by participating in Alan Cohen's in-person seminars, online courses, life coach training, or online subscription programs.

Inspirational Quote for the Day
An uplifting idea e-mailed to you each day (free)

Monthly e-Newsletter
Insightful articles and announcements of upcoming events (free)

From the Heart
YouTube live and recorded presentations
for practical spiritual living (free)

The Coaching Room
Live one-to-one online coaching with Alan (free)

Wisdom for Today
A daily inspirational message subscription service
with a lesson for each day of the year

Live Webinars
Interactive programs on topics relevant to spirituality,
self-empowerment, and holistic living

Online Courses
In-depth experiential exploration of healing, relationships,
prosperity, prayer, metaphysics, and stress management

Life Coach Training
Become a certified professional holistic life coach or enhance
your career and personal life with coaching skills

A Course in Miracles Retreat
A residential program to empower you to master
the principles and skills of this life-changing course

For information about all of these offerings, and more, visit
www.alancohen.com

Printed in Great Britain
by Amazon

85071840R00176